Modern Latin American Literature: A Very Short Introduction

VERY SHORT INTRODUCTIONS are for anyone wanting a stimulating and accessible way in to a new subject. They are written by experts and have been published in more than 25 languages worldwide.

The series began in 1995 and now represents a wide variety of topics in history, philosophy, religion, science, and the humanities. The VSI library now contains 300 volumes—a Very Short Introduction to everything from ancient Egypt and Indian philosophy to conceptual art and cosmology—and will continue to grow in a variety of disciplines.

Very Short Introductions available now:

ADVERTISING Winston Fletcher
AFRICAN HISTORY John Parker and
 Richard Rathbone
AGNOSTICISM Robin Le Poidevin
AMERICAN IMMIGRATION
 David A. Gerber
AMERICAN POLITICAL PARTIES
 AND ELECTIONS L. Sandy Maisel
THE AMERICAN PRESIDENCY
 Charles O. Jones
ANARCHISM Colin Ward
ANCIENT EGYPT Ian Shaw
ANCIENT GREECE Paul Cartledge
ANCIENT PHILOSOPHY Julia Annas
ANCIENT WARFARE
 Harry Sidebottom
ANGELS David Albert Jones
ANGLICANISM Mark Chapman
THE ANGLO-SAXON AGE John Blair
THE ANIMAL KINGDOM
 Peter Holland
ANIMAL RIGHTS David DeGrazia
ANTISEMITISM Steven Beller
THE APOCRYPHAL GOSPELS
 Paul Foster
ARCHAEOLOGY Paul Bahn
ARCHITECTURE Andrew Ballantyne
ARISTOCRACY William Doyle
ARISTOTLE Jonathan Barnes
ART HISTORY Dana Arnold
ART THEORY Cynthia Freeland

ATHEISM Julian Baggini
AUGUSTINE Henry Chadwick
AUTISM Uta Frith
THE AZTECS Davíd Carrasco
BARTHES Jonathan Culler
BEAUTY Roger Scruton
BESTSELLERS John Sutherland
THE BIBLE John Riches
BIBLICAL ARCHAEOLOGY
 Eric H. Cline
BIOGRAPHY Hermione Lee
THE BLUES Elijah Wald
THE BOOK OF MORMON
 Terryl Givens
THE BRAIN Michael O'Shea
BRITISH POLITICS Anthony Wright
BUDDHA Michael Carrithers
BUDDHISM Damien Keown
BUDDHIST ETHICS Damien Keown
CANCER Nicholas James
CAPITALISM James Fulcher
CATHOLICISM Gerald O'Collins
THE CELL
 Terence Allen and Graham Cowling
THE CELTS Barry Cunliffe
CHAOS Leonard Smith
CHILDREN'S LITERATURE
 Kimberley Reynolds
CHOICE THEORY Michael Allingham
CHRISTIAN ART Beth Williamson
CHRISTIAN ETHICS D. Stephen Long

Available soon:

For more information visit our web site

www.oup.co.uk/general/vsi/

Roberto González Echevarría

MODERN LATIN AMERICAN LITERATURE

A Very Short Introduction

OXFORD
UNIVERSITY PRESS

OXFORD
UNIVERSITY PRESS

Oxford University Press, Inc., publishes works that further
Oxford University's objective of excellence
in research, scholarship, and education.

Oxford New York
Auckland   Cape Town   Dar es Salaam   Hong Kong   Karachi
Kuala Lumpur   Madrid   Melbourne   Mexico City   Nairobi
New Delhi   Shanghai   Taipei   Toronto

With offices in
Argentina   Austria   Brazil   Chile   Czech Republic   France   Greece
Guatemala   Hungary   Italy   Japan   Poland   Portugal   Singapore
South Korea   Switzerland   Thailand   Turkey   Ukraine   Vietnam

Published by Oxford University Press, Inc.
198 Madison Avenue, New York, NY 10016

www.oup.com

Library of Congress Cataloging-in-Publication Data
González Echevarría, Roberto.
Modern Latin American literature : a very short introduction /
Roberto González Echevarría.
p.   cm. — (Very short introductions)
Includes bibliographical references and index.
ISBN 978-0-19-975491-5 (pbk.)
1. Spanish American literature—History and criticism. I. Title.
PQ7081.G6315   2012
860.9'98—dc23   2011031494

3 5 7 9 8 6 4

Printed in Great Britain
by Ashford Colour Press Ltd., Gosport, Hants.
on acid-free paper

A la memoria de Octavio Corvalán,
maestro tucumano

Contents

List of illustrations

Acknowledgments

Nancy Toff, editor at Oxford, convinced me that writing this book was a worthy endeavor, and it has been that. Compressing more than two centuries of modern Latin American literature in such a brief space was a compelling challenge conceptually and rhetorically. The effort forced me to clarify to myself a number of issues; I hope that they are clear to the reader. I also had to subject the corpus of texts comprising modern Latin American literary history to the most severe assessment in terms of quality and influence. Evaluation is the least acknowledged and discussed practice in literary criticism, but the most prevalent. I am sure that some of my colleagues in the field will not agree with all of my choices and that many will lament bitterly some of the inevitable exclusions. I challenge them to perform a similar exercise in conciseness. I always say, anyway, that criticism is the start, not the end of a discussion. The general reader will be merrily oblivious to these quarrels. I hope that upon finishing the book he or she will be eager to read Latin American literature.

I have written this very brief introduction keenly aware that my learned colleague and dear friend Rolena Adorno was writing her own on colonial Latin American literature. We agreed to make Andrés Bello the hinge between the two volumes, so the reader of both will have two takes on the Venezuela polymath. I have consulted Rolena at every step and have been enriched by her vast erudition, intelligence, and good sense. She is not responsible for the errors that I still made in spite of her wise counsel.

Jennifer Darrell, a young scholar, has been a smart, diligent, and learned assistant throughout the whole process of writing the book. I cannot thank her enough for her help on all matters, including the procurement and selection of illustrations.

I began the book during spring break 2010, on the dining room table of our rented apartment in Anna Maria Island, Florida, as my resigned, supporting, and beloved wife, Isabel, looked on and often encouraged me to take a break. I continued it that summer during our two-week stay in Chile (Santiago and Concepción), where Roberto Hozven, my host, friend, and a professor at the Pontificia Universidad Católica de Chile, was a sharp interlocutor who challenged me on a number of choices and opinions. I am very grateful for his insights. I am also indebted to Gustavo Pérez-Firmat, of Columbia University, with whom I discussed (argued) about many points to my benefit and, I hope, that of the book.

Chapter 1
Introduction

In the 1960s, Latin American literature became known worldwide as never before; Jorge Luis Borges, Gabriel García Márquez, Julio Cortázar, Mario Vargas Llosa, Carlos Fuentes, Pablo Neruda, and Octavio Paz were incorporated into the culture of educated readers in the West. Miguel Angel Asturias, Neruda, García Márquez, and Paz received Nobel Prizes, and it has been said that García Márquez is today the most influential writer in China. In 2010 Vargas Llosa too was awarded the Nobel Prize. Outside the Spanish-speaking world, however, few know about the literary tradition from which these authors emerged.

Although Latin Americans had been writing for a long time, Latin American literature became conscious of itself in the 1850s, when a group of exiles and diplomats from several Latin American countries found each other in Paris, and decided to launch a journal and prepare critical editions of colonial texts that they considered to be the origin of their newly discovered literary tradition. This process of mutual recognition took place in the wake of independence from Spain and set in motion trends and practices that still endure today.

The first of those trends is that Latin American literature would become aware of itself as a continent-wide phenomenon, not just as an assemblage of national literatures, in times of political

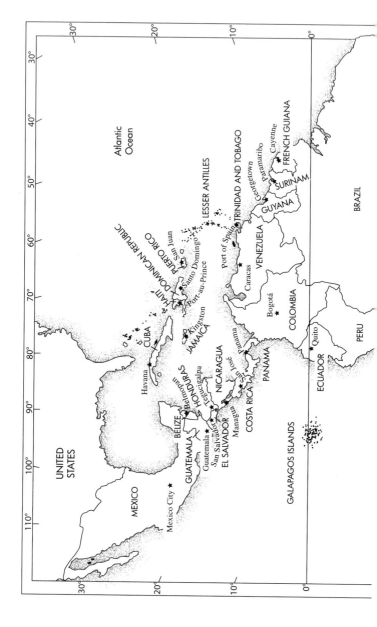

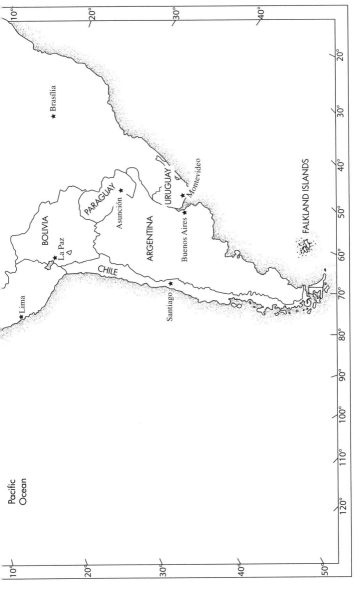

1. Contemporary Latin America.

change. The first was independence and its aftermath. The next crisis was provided by the Spanish-American War, which not only brought down what was left of the Spanish empire but also made manifest the chasm existing between the Hispanic and the Anglo-American worlds, and between Spain and its former colonies. This feeling of cultural difference would produce Modernismo, the first literary movement to emerge from Latin America. In the early twentieth century, the end of World War I and the Soviet and Mexican revolutions produced the avant-garde, which generated a plethora of literary production, chiefly in poetry and to a lesser degree in prose fiction. The catastrophic First World War confirmed the breakdown of the European ideals and aspirations developed during the nineteenth century, the heyday of new scientific discoveries, and unbridled imperial expansion.

The West was clearly in crisis. This brought about a sense of liberation in the arts, including the European ones themselves, which spread throughout Latin America, where avant-garde movements proliferated and followed one another, encouraging much literary activity. During the Spanish Civil War (1936–39) writers from all over the world, among them many Latin Americans, converged on the Peninsula to fight for the Republic. The meeting of Spanish and Latin American writers, particularly poets, fostered a sense of common political and aesthetic purpose among all and brought about what amounted to a golden age in Spanish-language poetry. In the 1960s the Cuban Revolution, together with a general trend toward decolonization, sparked the movement in the Latin American novel that came to be known as the Boom.

While Latin American writers feel part of a continent-wide literature in moments of historical crisis, each Latin American country has its own national literature, nurtured and promoted by its government, with local specific traits and celebrated writers. Because of the centralized bureaucratic nature of the Latin American republics, writers and other intellectuals are often functionaries of the state, occupying positions as exalted as ambassadorships or as modest as teachers and bureaucrats. The major national literatures developed in the larger countries, particularly those that were the seats of viceroyalties during the colonial period (Mexico, Peru, the River Plate area), though Colombia, Chile, and Cuba have thriving national literatures, the latter because Havana was the meeting port of the biannual fleets that connected the Spanish Empire to the metropolis. Size or importance, in any case, does not assure the emergence of significant authors. Tiny Nicaragua saw the birth of Rubén Darío in 1867, the most influential poet in the Spanish language since Garcilaso de la Vega (1501–36).

The second trend that those writers and intellectuals started in Paris was that Latin American artists would continue to gravitate to the French capital and, whenever possible, run their literary and artistic movements from that city. Given that there are nineteen Latin American countries spread over a vast, fragmented territory, there is no logical metropolis for them to meet, like New York for the Americans or London for the English. Besides that geographical reality, Paris meant freedom from the Spanish tradition and an affirmation of a cosmopolitanism that was lacking in Spain. Latin American intellectuals and artists have tended to be French oriented, and very few of the major ones did not speak French; most do to this day.

With such a continental, cosmopolitan orientation, Latin American literature also affirmed a quality that separated it from the literature of the United States, with which it would nevertheless sustain relations throughout the nineteenth and twentieth centuries, but from which it differs substantially. Latin American literature has tended to be urban, of the city, not exalting the countryside and nature as sources of inspiration and ideal sites for its production, as in Anglo-American literature. Nature, in the form of jungles or endless plains, appears as a menacing yet alluring presence, the keeper of dark secrets about individual and collective identity; it is rarely idealized as a pastoral setting.

A third enduring practice that those writers began in Paris was the creation of a journal to promote the philosophical and aesthetic accord of their group. The history of modern Latin American literature can be, and has been, written following the emergence of such journals throughout the continent. The first was not the one founded in Paris but Andrés Bello's *El repertorio americano* (1826–27), which the Venezuelan founded during his exile in London. But this was an individual, not a collective, project. Many, like the one in Paris, followed: *Sur* in Buenos Aires, *Orígenes* in Havana, *Contemporáneos* in Mexico City, and *Asomante* in San Juan, Puerto Rico. There are many others, such as the current *Letras libres* in Mexico. For the most part these journals have been self-sustaining. Yet others have been supported by governments, like *Casa de las Américas* in Havana, which was created by Fidel Castro's communist dictatorship as part of its cultural propaganda campaign.

Another trend the Paris-based, nineteenth-century Latin American writers started was the effort to incorporate texts from the colonial period into their sense of a shared literary past, an origin. As Romantics, they endeavored to create a new tradition with a significant source of its own, like those the European literatures had found in "national" epics such as the *Poema del Mío Cid*, *Chanson de Roland*, the *Nibelungenlied*, and *Beowulf*. This was complicated in Latin America by the fact that colonial works were produced during Spain's overseas domination, and many were written by authors born in Spain. The solution to this problem was to stress that the chronicles of the discovery and conquest of America, which had an epic quality, related deeds occurring within the territory of what would become Latin America. They also called attention to the fact that poets and artists of what came to be known as the Barroco de Indias, a strong seventeenth-century New World trend, emphasized their being American as their essential Baroque oddity. In many instances these colonial antecedents are enabling fictions of considerable interest for the moment in which they were invented.

Those founding Latin American authors had in common with their North American counterparts the wish to create a literature whose newness reflected that of the New World in which it was conceived, a feature that has continued until the present. The conceit of novelty would in the future be predicated on the presence in the Americas of peoples who were alien to Western history, whether because they were natives of the New World or, as with the descendants of Africans, because their forebears were not of European origin. In various guises, this conceit has endured until today, propped up by the contradiction that the language and the literary conventions in which Latin American literature is written are both thoroughly Western. Walt Whitman's titanic quest to write a personal and collective epic naming the new realities of the New World found echoes in the Latin American poetry of the likes of Neruda and in García Márquez' fictions. Borges' answer to the conundrum Latin Americans faced wanting to create a new tradition, yet rooted in a Western one, is that Latin Americans should simply assume the Western tradition as theirs but to do so without reverence, to feel free and unencumbered by it. The struggle with this issue has been a topic in the Latin American essay dealing with the issue of identity, national and Latin American, with different inflections determined by the writer's particular region of origin.

But what is Latin America, and how did it come to be so named? The Spanish empire endowed its possessions in the New World with a remarkable and resilient unity thanks to three institutions they exported and promoted aggressively: the Spanish language, the Roman Catholic Church, and the law. The three have remained at the core of Latin American culture, which is solidly attached to the West through these and other institutions, such as education. (There is in certain Latin American literary works, like the *Canto general* and *Cien años de soledad*, a totalizing view of Latin America that betrays a nostalgia for the old Spanish Empire, and ultimately a Catholic universalism that harkens back to the Roman Empire). Independence did not shatter that unity, which is the reason why, in spite of there being nineteen Spanish-speaking nations in Latin America, there is an overarching Latin American cultural tradition and sustained intellectual and artistic exchange among all of them, and also with Spain.

Latin America was called "Latin" by the French when they embarked in their catastrophic imperial venture in Mexico in the middle of the nineteenth century, with the intention of filling the void left by the Spanish after independence. The French appealed to the common Latin origin of French and Spanish to forge an alliance that would counter Anglo-America—that is, the United States. Of course, the name "Latin America" is in those terms inappropriate, not only because there are many in Latin America who are not descendants of Europeans but also because the remote Latin origin of the language is a philological myth with little or no political currency. English is a Germanic language, but no one would think of calling natives of the United States and Canada Germanic Americans. But as inaccurate and awkward as it is, Latin America has stuck as the name for the territories of the former Spanish empire (not without some competition from Hispanoamérica, Iberoamérica, and even Indoamérica). Since the modern sense of being Latin American dates roughly to when the name was given to the region, it is not altogether wrong to continue using it, always recognizing that no name ever properly reflects the essence of the region, nation, or ethnic group that it designates.

What about Brazil? Brazilian literature is, second to that of the United States, the richest national literature in the Americas, and it has had substantial though intermittent exchanges with the literatures of the rest of the Americas. But it is a literature of its own, written in a cognate but different language than Spanish, and cannot be simply lumped together under one rubric with the literatures of Spanish-speaking America, even though it certainly is a Latin American literature.

Chapter 2

Poetry from Romanticism to Modernismo: Bello to Darío

Poetry is the genre to first register changes in artistic sensibility, and the new American inflection of Latin American literature that emerged at the beginning of the nineteenth century was initially expressed in verse. The first poets to manifest the change were still under the sway of neoclassicism, which made the representation of specifically new-world conditions difficult; their prosodic habits and range of allusions were determined by the imitation of Greek and Roman models, as adapted by eighteenth-century European poetry, particularly Spanish.

Throughout the nineteenth century Latin American poetry struggled to achieve a genuine expression, to shed a language predicated on European realities and modes of thought. This effort was more often than not allied to the battle first for political independence from Spain, and later for the discovery of national and continental styles of government attuned to the geographic and demographic characteristics of the various regions.

No poetry could be more closely associated with independence than that of the Ecuadorian José Joaquín Olmedo (1790–1847), whose most significant poem (definitive edition 1826) was a hymn dedicated to the liberator Simón Bolívar and his victory over the Spanish at Junín (Peru). This epic-like ode, titled "La victoria de Junín: canto a Bolívar" (The Victory at Junín: A Song to Bolívar), very much in the neoclassical style, is an ambitious poem whose historical sweep encompasses the whole of the Latin American past from pre-Columbian times to the date of the battle it celebrates.

The poem had been commissioned by Bolívar himself, with the proviso that it leave him out, which was of course impossible. In imitation of Roman models, mostly Virgil, Olmedo's poem focuses on the heroic figure of the Liberator, whose grandiose plans for the foundation of a large new nation, Gran Colombia—which would encompass today's Venezuela, Panama, Colombia, Peru, Bolivia, and Chile—rivals that of the establishment of Rome as sung by the *Aeneid.* The din of battle is evoked by resounding alliterations and onomatopoeias, and its ennobling quality highlighted by allusions to classical mythology, which places this American event at the core of Western history. But the most daring twist in the poem was caused by the pressure of actual historical events.

The battle of Junín, at which Bolívar played a starring role, took place on August 6, 1824, but the decisive battle of Ayacucho (Peru), which put an end to Spanish rule in South America, was not fought until December 9 of that year. At Ayacucho the victorious commander was the youthful Antonio José de Sucre, not Bolívar, who was not present. This put Olmedo in a quandary, for he needed the Liberator to be the hero; besides, his poem extolling the battle of Junín was already completed and, in good neoclassical fashion, observed the unities of place and time. Olmedo's grand solution, one in keeping with epic tradition, was to have Huaina Cápac, the last of the Inca emperors, appear to the combatants in a vision, prophesying the forthcoming battle of Ayacucho, at which their work would be finished. The story of the Incas allows Olmedo to drag in the whole history of the colonial period, redolent with the abuses visited upon the Indians by the Spaniards, whom he excoriates, with the exception of Fray Bartolomé de las Casas, their defender. He envisions a heaven in which Bolívar will dwell with the Inca emperors.

Bolívar was Olmedo's first critic. The Liberator was not pleased with the inclusion of Huaina Cápac, whom he thought overwhelmed the poem with his somewhat garrulous presence. Bolívar obviously did not like to share the limelight. Still, "La victoria de Junín: canto a Bolívar" is a remarkable modern epic, set at the foundation of new nations, as epics are supposed to be, with an elevated tone and style commensurate with its grandiose theme. It is crammed with classical allusions, there are hyperbatons (unusual word order) that echo Latin syntax, the rhetoric is to some extent oratorical, and the lexicon can be obscure.

The neoclassical mood is felt not just in these features but also in the longing for peace and tranquility expressed as the desire to transform swords into plows. Yet, there are moments when Olmedo's poetic gift overcomes these limitations and comes through in delicate lines, as when he says that the monuments erected by man's vanity "are scorned by time which / with its delicate wing touches them, bringing them down." There is also the joyful mention of American fruit (tamarinds, pineapples), with their euphonious names and sensual evocations, which together with the insertion of America into universal history lend the poem the air of a fresh beginning, a persistent and defining topic in modern Latin American literature.

The Venezuelan Andrés Bello (1781–1865) was the first modern Latin American intellectual and poet. A polymath, Bello was a grammarian, philosopher, lawmaker, academic, translator, essayist, and poet. He wrote a grammar of the Spanish language, helped draft the Chilean judicial code, founded the University of Chile, was an advisor to Bolívar, founded an important journal, *El repertorio americano*, and published influential poetry in the neoclassical style. Bello straddled the Enlightenment and Romanticism. He went to England in 1810 as an aid to Bolívar and stayed in London until 1829.

This was a fruitful and formative period of his life, during which he devoted himself to the study of languages, literature,

AL

PUEBLO AMERICANO.

LOS EDITORES.

2. Frontispiece (*above*) and title page (*opposite*) of the first issue of *El repertorio americano*, the journal Andrés Bello of Venezuela published in London in 1826.

EL

REPERTORIO

AMERICANO.

TOMO PRIMERO.

OCTUBRE DE 1826.

LONDRES:

EN LA LIBRERIA DE BOSSANGE, BARTHÉS I LOWELL,

14, GREAT MARLBOROUGH STREET.

1826

philosophy, and the law. He came into contact with early Romantic nature poetry and translated Byron. But his inclinations were neoclassical. Between 1829 and 1865 he lived in Chile, devoting himself to drafting Chilean law, organizing the university, serving as its first president, a post he held until his death. In that period he engaged in polemics with the Argentine exile Domingo Faustino Sarmiento, who was imbued in French Romanticism and found Bello too neoclassical.

Bello was also a Romantic of sorts, but he had imbibed Romanticism at its English source, although he did write an adaptation of Victor Hugo's "Prayer for All." Bello's Romanticism was philosophical more than literary. In his splendid new Spanish grammar he argued that Spanish grammar ought not to be slavishly modeled after that of Latin and dismissed the notion that the language as spoken in Spain should be the model of correctness. This Americanism shows Bello's Romantic appreciation of the native mind, also evident in his admonitions in the speech to commemorate the founding of the University of Chile, that American science ought to be bold and innovative, not restricted by European traditions, which should be respected but not copied heedlessly.

Bello also urged the study of native histories by going to the sources in Spanish colonial chronicles, reaching all the way back to Columbus. This conscious appropriation of colonial texts as part of the Latin American tradition was liberating and foundational in that it eschewed the rejection of the mother country in a spirit of reconciliation after the achievement of independence.

This innovative spirit is nearly, though not completely, absent from Bello's poetry. His best-known poems are his two *silvas*, known by their renaissance-style stanza consisting of verses of eleven and seven syllables. "Alocución a la poesía" (An Address to Poetry, 1823), part of an unfinished, ambitious poem that he planned to title "America," is a call for poetry to abandon the European courts and come to America to find originality. The most important silva was the other, "A la agricultura de la zona tórrida" (Agriculture in the Torrid Zone, 1826), which he was never able to amalgamate with "Alocución" because it had a different tone and spirit. He sings not so much to nature as a wondrous source of mystery and poetry but to the exploitation of America's bountiful nature for the benefit of society. He does this in perfectly measured verses overflowing with classical allusions, in a style that is very much that of Horace and Virgil. Bello's tone is didactic and at worst preachy.

But there are stirring moments in the silva, when the evocation of American nature overcomes his neoclassical restraint. In these passages, like Olmedo, Bello revels in the exotic names of American fruits and plants. And there are lines in which the true poet in Bello filters through the classical prosody and rhetoric, as when he refers to the sun, drawn by the torrid zone as "in love," or draws this lovely pair of contraries to describe nature as "where the flower charms, the thorn pricks." There is pathos also in the broad historical perspective, as when he writes that "Sated of Iberian blood already rest / the ghosts of Atahualpa and Moctezuma." Bello's versatility and Pan-Americanism are foundational.

A decisive step toward a Romantic poetry freed from neoclassical conventions was taken by the Cuban José María Heredia (1803–39), although he remained attached to neoclassical verse forms. Precocious, Heredia was steeped in Latin literature in his childhood and began to write poetry in his adolescence; he had already published major poems before he reached the age of twenty. In contrast to Olmedo's and Bello's, Heredia's country, Cuba, had not yet attained its independence, and he declared early in life his opposition to the Spanish regime. His activities made of him an exile, first in the United States and later in Mexico, where he established himself and produced most of his work. Hence Heredia became, with Bello, the first of many Latin American poets whose exiled condition turned into a significant theme of his writing; being an exile was for him a poetic stance or persona.

This state dovetailed with the Romantic feelings of alienation that dominated Western art and literature in the early nineteenth century. Heredia also developed into an activist of note, a conspirator persecuted by the Spanish authorities, and he became involved in Mexican politics at the highest levels. But his most important contribution was to poetry: his are among the first truly poetic Latin American verses of the modern era.

Heredia wrote an ode to Bolívar in a tone reminiscent of Olmedo and Bello in which he reviews disparagingly the centuries of Spanish colonial rule and celebrates the Liberator's role in bringing about independence. He also composed an ode to Cholula's *teocalli*, or pyramid, the monumental mound on which stood a massive Aztec temple, in which he decried the cruelty of the Indians' rituals and praised the prominence of the site while ruefully remarking on how time has turned it into ruins.

These poems, written, like all of Heredia's, in a neoclassic style and versification, distinguish themselves from those of his contemporaries and predecessors only by their emotional tone, which makes them more personal. Heredia's innovation is precisely the poetic voice's engagement with the subject matter of the poems, particularly nature, and more specifically a turbulent nature that reflects the unsettled state of the poetic self. This is not Wordsworth's nature, with its gentle call to self-reflection, but a nature in turmoil, shaken to the foundations of the earth and awakening in the poet sentiments of fear, awe, and visions of an all-powerful, raging God. The best of these is a classic of Latin American poetry, Heredia's ode "Niágara" (1824).

The Niagara poem, with its dynamic depiction of the angry waters as they plunge and swirl violently, is a veritable tour de force. The waterfall arouses the poet's dormant inspiration, launching him on a meditation about his own distressed inner world and generating sublime visions of beauty. The agitated northern landscape, filled with impressive pine trees, stirs in him feelings of nostalgia for

Cuba, whose landscape, dotted with swaying palms bathed by the bright tropical sun, he lovingly evokes. This reminiscence inspires the most beautiful stanza of the poem and three truly remarkable lines, when Heredia writes of the "the delicious palm trees / that on the plains of my burning motherland / are born from the sun to smile and grow." Heredia is the first Romantic Latin American poet worthy of note and, to some, the movement's most important figure.

In the south, specifically Argentina, Romanticism entered in a militant way. Esteban Echeverría (1805–51) was the mediator. At twenty, he went to Paris and stayed for four years, during which he was dazzled by Musset, Lamartine, Dumas, Hugo, and other French poets who were at the height of their creativity. Upon returning to Buenos Aires, Echeverría not only began to publish poems in a Romantic tone and style but also founded the Asociación de Mayo (May, after the month in which Argentina attained independence), a literary club to promote the new movement. The club, which soon spread its influence to the provinces and to Uruguay, was also a political organization with liberal ideas that opposed the dictatorship of Juan Manuel de Rosas. A liberal and pre-Marxist socialist, Echeverría was vigorously involved in the opposition and eventually died in exile, in Montevideo.

With his journey to Paris and political and literary activities, Echeverría became the prototypical Latin American writer and intellectual, a model followed by many until the present. The Asociación de Mayo had its counterparts in other Latin American countries: gatherings of writers, mostly poets, who met to exchange ideas, read their works in progress, and conspire against the authorities.

Echeverría was not a major poet, but he was highly influential nevertheless. He is remembered mostly for a long, narrative poem, "La cautiva" (The Captive Woman), which appeared in his volume *Las rimas* (1837). The legend tells the story of Brian and

María during the fierce wars fought by the Argentine state against the Indians who roamed the country's vast plains, the *pampas*. Savage and bent on exacting revenge on the whites, the Indians fight ferociously and the soldiers respond in kind. Brian is severely wounded and left nearly for dead, but María courageously drags him to safety in the night, crossing turbulent rivers and raging prairie fires. He finally dies, and when Maria is rescued by the soldiers she is told that the Indians have also slit their son's throat. She too dies, and the couple is buried in a tomb graced by a cross and an *ombú* tree that grows robustly as if to mark their heroism. The tale is like an Ovidian metamorphosis.

While this melodramatic tale is somewhat overstated and even somewhat trite, Echeverría's poetry exhibits some innovative traits that would leave a mark. There is, in contrast to Bello, Olmedo, and Heredia, an absence of classical allusions as well as the abandonment of classic metrical forms in favor of shorter, traditional verse of the kind used by popular poetry. More importantly, perhaps, there is the presence of the Argentine landscape, a specifically American setting, with its typical flora and fauna, whose vernacular names—*ombú*, for instance—are regional words derived from Indian languages. But the most impressive feature of Echeverría's poem is the feeling of the infinite provoked by the measureless *pampas*, called "el desierto," but there is no sand in them; instead they are grassy plains extending to the horizon. Echeverría's Romantic sublime emerges from this sense of cosmic emptiness in which the self finds no bearings: "The desert, / measureless, wide open / and mysterious at his feet."

By the middle of the nineteenth century there emerged a group of poets, critics, and scholars who began to conceive of a Latin American literature, following the initiative of Bello. These individuals gathered in Paris and in Latin American cities in countries other than their own because they were sent there as diplomats by their governments, or because they were in exile from dictatorial regimes. They were Romantics, many of them Argentinean, but also Peruvian, Chilean, Venezuelan, and Colombian. Their sense of being part of one continental cultural and political domain is evident by the collections of essays and poems they published, containing authors from Latin American countries other than the editor's.

The Colombian José María Torres Caicedo (1830–89), a diplomat, essayist, and critic who lived in Paris around the middle of the century, was involved with many other Latin Americans, about whom he wrote in a series of books called *Ensayos biográficos y de crítica literaria sobre los principales publicistas, historiadores, poetas y literatos de América Latina* (Biographical and Critical Essays on the Chief Authors, Historians, Poets, and Men of Letters from Latin America). Torres Caicedo also brought out a journal in Paris called *El Correo de Ultramar* (The Overseas Courier), where he published articles on his fellow Latin American writers. The Chilean Diego Barros Arana (1830–1907) planned a *Bibliotheca Americana: Collection d'Ouvrages inédits ou rares sur l'Amérique* (American Library: A Collection of Unpublished or Rare Works on America) in which he attempted to publish (in Paris) editions of sixteenth- and seventeenth-century works—though the only one that appeared was *Purén indómito* (Indomitable Purén), by Captain Fernando Alvarez de Toledo.

Of all these books the most significant was the anthology *América poética*, by Juan Maria Gutiérrez (1809–78), a brilliant Argentine from Echeverría's Buenos Aires group. It was published in Valparaíso, Chile, where he was in exile. In a gesture proclaiming his desire to establish an American poetic tradition, Gutiérrez opens *América poética* with Bello's "Alocución a la poesía," as a kind of defining epigraph. Romanticism still had to produce a few more important figures and the finest Latin American poem of the nineteenth century: José Hernández's gaucho epic, *Martín Fierro*.

Among the many Romantic writers was the Cuban Gertrudis Gómez de Avellaneda (1814–73), the first important woman poet to emerge in the region since the Mexican Sor Juana Inés de la Cruz in the seventeenth century. Gómez de Avellaneda, born in the provincial town of Puerto Príncipe, today Camagüey, to a Cuban mother and a Spanish father, left Cuba at age twenty-two and spent most of her productive years as a poet, novelist, and quite successful playwright in Spain. A passionate woman who had a daughter out of wedlock, married twice, and is known to have had several lovers, Gómez de Avellaneda was a Romantic with a restrained style, probably the result of her readings of Spanish neoclassical poets in her youth. She achieved recognition in Spain, whose literature claims her as its own, but she was denied admittance to the Spanish Academy because she was a woman.

Her verse exhibits academic polish, and she used a variety of meters quite skillfully. She did return to Cuba in 1859 and was triumphantly received by the island's literati and cultural authorities. Gómez de Avellaneda always expressed longings for Cuba, which she considered her country, and wrote movingly of her yearnings for the island, most memorably in a perfect sonnet she claims to have improvised at twenty-two upon boarding ship to leave in 1836: "Al partir" (On my departure). She wrote a moving elegy for Heredia in which she speaks of Cuba's mourning for the loss of its bard and patriot. Although the daughter of a Spanish military officer and married to another military man, Gómez de Avellaneda was obviously in favor of Cuba's independence, and she wrote a solemn sonnet to George Washington, whom she celebrates as the liberator of his country. She returned to Spain in 1864.

Gómez de Avellaneda´s poetry exhibited a formal polish unusual for a mid-century Romantic. Her poems "A él" (For him) tell of an unrequited love for a man who was cool to her affections and eventually broke with her. She expresses deep feelings of attraction for him and disappointment rather than despair because of the separation. Gómez de Avellaneda was not an erotic poet, though she wrote ardent love letters. Her poem "A la poesía" (To Poetry) reveals a conception of her art as the guide to God in his creation of the world and that which endows nature with beauty and meaning. Hers is a belief in the powers of poetry that sounds more neoplatonic, pantheistic, and secular than Christian or Romantic. Gómez de Avellaneda sings to an abstract God in terms that are moving more because of their beauty than their passion. In the dull firmament of Spanish nineteenth-century letters she was a bright star.

José Hernández´s *El gaucho Martín Fierro* (1872) is unique in nineteenth-century poetry not only because of its epic quality but also because it achieved something that poets of the century yearned for but rarely achieved: a truly broad readership and incorporation into nationalistic myths. Hernández (1834–86) sold 100,000 copies of his book-length poem, which was distributed throughout Argentina, even in country stores in the rural regions in which the poem is set and its hero roamed. Hernández's gaucho voice was recognized and incorporated by real gauchos. This is a rare triumph for a modern poet. Hernández was able to mimic the speech of gauchos and to imitate the poetry of the *payadores*, country minstrels who sang their exploits–he had grown up in the provinces listening to them. Hernández had a keen ear for the archaic speech of the gauchos. Many rural terms come from the horse and cattle culture of the roaming gauchos, who seemed to be one with their mounts and hated to be off of them. The gauchos are like American cowboys, but they are more nomadic and isolated. In fact, they cherish their freedom, something that is at the core of Hernández's poem and feeds into its romantic ideology.

Martín Fierro has a very appropriate name: Martín comes from Mars, god of war, and *fierro* is old Spanish for "iron." He is tough but also artistic: the poem is a song he sings like a "lonesome bird to console himself." It is a sententious song, in which outrage and love of the land and the gaucho's way of life are celebrated in the popular poetry stanzas, using rural tropes and words that sound folksy, but never maudlin, apologetic, or condescending. Fierro's sorrows were caused by the government, which conscripted him into the army to fight the Indians who were still controlling considerable Argentine territory; as a result of having been forced into the army he lost his house, wife, and child, all of which he had to abandon. He becomes a deserter and a criminal, having "had" to kill a black man in a dance brawl. He is a quintessential romantic outlaw, a fugitive from justice; that is, from the nation-state that wants to turn him into its soldier.

Hernández's resentful hero embodies virtues that national mythmaking wanted to claim as the Argentineans' essential character traits: independence, courage, stoicism. Hernández not only created an Argentine national myth and gave shape to a strand of literature that would reach the work of Jorge Luis Borges, but he also produced the first Latin American literary myth—an enduring one at that. In a second part, *La vuelta de Martín Fierro* (The Return of Martín Fierro, 1879), Hernández has the gaucho return to the fold and, in a didactic mood, join in the effort of nation building. Romantic ideology created the medieval epic monuments that presumably stand at the beginning of European national languages and literatures (*Poema del Mío Cid, Chanson de Roland*), and Hernández endowed Argentine and Latin American literature with a modern epic of its own. He did so just as Latin American literature was about to produce its first literary movement, Modernismo, which would be the gateway to twentieth-century literature.

Modernismo has a clear beginning: Rubén Darío's *Azul . . .* , published in Valparaiso, Chile, in 1888. Darío (1867–1916) was born in Metapa, Nicaragua, and named Félix Rubén García Sarmiento, of parents of Spanish, Indian, and African blood. He later changed his name to the shorter, euphonious Rubén Darío, incorporating a patronymic that his father's family had used—it also has classical echoes, of course. He was raised in the politically and intellectually active Nicaraguan city of León. Darío acquired a vast and deep cultural education during his childhood and

LA VUELTA

DE

MARTIN FIERRO

POR

JOSÉ HERNANDEZ

PRIMERA EDICION, ADORNADA CON DIEZ LAMINAS

SE VENDE EN TODAS LAS LIBRERIAS DE BUENOS AIRES

Depósito central: LIBRERIA DEL PLATA, Calle Tacuari, 17

1879

3. Title page of the second part of *Martín Fierro*, a popular gaucho epic published by José Hernández of Argentina in 1879.

adolescence, and immersed himself in French poetry. He read avidly and learned nearly all of the metrical and rhyme schemes of Spanish poetry, the whole range of it. As a poet, he became a Mozart of Spanish verse, using thirty-seven different metrical lines and 136 stanza forms in his career; some were of his own invention. After publishing in local newspapers, Darío moved to Chile in search of better possibilities.

The prospect of becoming so well-read on the margins of the Spanish-speaking world was due to the uniformity of language and culture imposed on its empire by the Spanish crown as well as by advances in technology, particularly communications. These replaced the order enforced by the imperial bureaucracy. Gutenberg's revolution had truly exploded when steam power was coupled to the printing press in the nineteenth century, making books available in large numbers for the first time. Steamboats carried books as well as their authors across oceans, making the impact of a literary movement nearly instantaneous and widespread. It was these ships that made possible the meeting of Latin American writers and intellectuals in Paris in the 1850s. The transatlantic cable carried copy to newspapers all over the world. Poets living in New York or Paris could publish in Buenos Aires' *La Nación* or Santiago de Chile's *El Mercurio*. Darío's fame, and his own person, traveled quickly throughout Latin America and Spain. He became the first Spanish-language literary celebrity, and his influence spread not just to other Latin American countries but to Spain itself, where Darío lived for a number of years. Prolific, charismatic, with a penchant for decadent life, Darío was congenial with politicians, some of them minor dictators, to the dismay of his admirers.

Azul . . . , a slender book of 134 pages, privately printed, became the modern turning point in Spanish literary history on both sides of the Atlantic. Some of the early reactions to it were hostile. The major Spanish thinker and poet Miguel de Unamuno first said that a feather stuck out of Darío's hat, a slur about his Indian background, while Marcelino Menéndez y Pelayo, the most influential Spanish critic and scholar of all time, stopped his history of Latin American poetry (the first, published in 1893) in the 1880s, exactly at the point that Darío and Modernismo began to make their mark. But the Nicaraguan had had the nerve to send *Azul* . . . to the powerful Spanish writer and critic Juan Valera. Valera wielded his considerable influence as an author, critic, and member of the Spanish Academy of the Language to launch the young poet's career with two "letters" about his book, which were printed as a prologue in later editions of *Azul* . . . Though critical of Darío's fondness for French poets, Valera recognized his genius and predicted a bright future for the Nicaraguan.

Azul . . . is a mixture of poetry and prose (short stories) in an exquisite style evoking a timeless, mythic world of nymphs, princesses, and artists in pursuit of an aesthetic ideal, an ideal of beauty that would restore to the world its lost unity and harmony. This is art's highest mission, and Darío espoused it with religious fervor. The artists who appear in *Azul* . . . are constantly frustrated in their efforts by mindless, crass aristocrats lacking good taste. There is a rift between the ideal pursued and the possibility of its attainment, a constant in Darío's work that accounts for its melancholic undertones. But there are no fissures in the execution of the poems or prose pieces, which seem to have purged from their discourse anything vulgar or worn out, and to bring refined poetry to levels of unimaginable perfection. But in all its perfection there is always a sense of longing, wonder, and even self-doubt. This is why Darío chose the swan as the emblem of his poetry: the bird combined artistic purity in his shape and white feathers with the wistful question mark of its curved neck. Darío drew heavily from classical mythology as well as pre-Columbian myths and the whole spectrum of Western history and culture, which he seemed to have at his fingertips.

In all of this Darío was moving away from Spanish Romanticism, with its maudlin, rhetorical, and hackneyed ways, with emotion overpowering the sense of beauty, and from all of Romanticism in fact. Modernismo sought to freeze in beautiful forms the hot thrust of romantic poetry. This was its "modernity," to have the self's woes submit to the force of poetic language, in the same way that nature was being subjected and given shape by science and technology in the second half of the nineteenth century. Even in lines of Darío's best-known, hence most criticized and parodied poem, "Sonatina," one finds this shaping process: "The princess is sad, what could be wrong with the princess? / Sighs escape from her strawberry mouth / which has lost its laughter, which has lost its color." Sighs, emotion issuing from within the princess, her inner self, are exhaled through strawberry-colored lips. "Strawberry mouth" is an elegant, though shocking twist that draws attention to the mouth's shape and color rather than to the source or contents of the sighs. We no longer care about what is wrong with the princess, her state of mind, but only about the beauty of the strawberry-colored lips through which the sighs emanate. The entire poem, with its longing to become music—it is called, after all, *sonatina*—is contained in that daring trope by which the mouth, the source of language and meaning, turns into a spring of color and flavor that, because of Darío's genius, can easily go unnoticed.

Darío's poetic career unfolded in two halves. The first, the aestheticist Darío, turned into its convex mirror image in the second, the more reflexive and reflective Darío—the "deep Darío," was the old cliché. The break between the two was announced, according to an earlier school of Darío readers, by the opening line of his 1905 work *Cantos de vida y esperanza* (Songs of Life and Hope): "I am the one who only yesterday was saying." The self-critical stance of the *Cantos* led many to speak of two Daríos, one enthralled by empty verbal pyrotechnics and another beset by profound personal, poetic, and political anxieties. The two Daríos are in fact the same Darío using different poetic conventions to say the same things. A new Darío did emerge in his later poetry, as his work took on a more political tone, reflecting his feeling that his stature entitled him to speak for the Spanish world.

It was in 1898, with the Spanish-American War, that Darío's and Modernismo's poetics gelled. While he and other Latin Americans applauded the liberation of Cuba, Puerto Rico, and other colonies from the crumbling Spanish Empire, they became keenly concerned about the emergence of the United States as a new imperial power. To Darío and the Modernistas, the Spanish world seemed helpless in the face of American expansionism, not only in politics but, even more importantly, also in culture. Catholic countries that traced their cultural and religious roots back to Rome would now be taken over by a colonial power that was Anglo-Saxon and Protestant, and that espoused a pragmatic approach to material progress, which was dangerously at odds with their culture. Darío expressed these concerns in a rousing ode "A Roosevelt" where he speaks on behalf of an America that *still* prays to Jesus and speaks Spanish. The "still" shows Darío's fear for the future of Latin America. He calls the United States in this poem "the future invader." The United States had, in fact, invaded Mexico repeatedly by that time.

A Modernista poet who was instrumental in starting the Cuban War of Independence in 1895, which turned into the Spanish-American War three years later, was José Martí. Martí (1853–95) was born in Havana of Spanish parents and at an early age heard the call to free his motherland from the metropolis. Still in his teens when he was sentenced to forced labor for his conspiratorial activities, he was subsequently exiled to Spain, where he continued the struggle, began writing poetry, and acquired a law degree. A martyr who became the most revered Cuban patriot, Martí was a prolific journalist, orator, and poet whose renown spread throughout Latin America, where he traveled, spoke, and published extensively. He settled in New York City and set about organizing Cuban exiles and veterans of the failed independence war of 1868–78. He succeeded and managed to land in eastern Cuba with an armed party in the early spring of 1895. On May 19, at a skirmish in Dos Ríos, he was felled by bullets. Fulfilling the longed-for destiny of Romantic poets like Byron to die for a cause,

Martí became the model for Latin American revolutionaries, particularly writers and intellectuals. He was only forty-two when he died, but he left behind a voluminous oeuvre, particularly in the form of speeches, essays, newspapers stories (some in English), chronicles, and poetry.

Martí did not have the time, because of his early death and his frenzied political activity, to publish a vast and influential corpus of poetry. Only two slim volumes of poetry were printed during his lifetime—*Ismaelillo* (1882) and *Versos sencillos* (1891)—but he did attain renown as a poet because his works appeared in periodicals in New York and throughout Latin America. *Ismaelillo*, a tender book about the son Martí´s estranged wife had taken with her back to Cuba, contains some striking poems revealing the poet's turbulent feelings and longings. *Versos sencillos*, made up of quatrains of deceptive simplicity and sounding very much like traditional Spanish poetry, became Martí´s most acclaimed book. His posthumous *Versos libres* is the more daring of his two collections and the one that contains his best mature poetry. Some poems in this book, like "Amor de ciudad grande" (Love in the City) uncannily announce the work of avant-garde poets of the next century. Martí was exposed in New York to a modern metropolis. He had also been reading Poe and Whitman (about whom he wrote) in English, a poetry freed from the prosodic and rhetorical constraints of Spanish and French poetry. *Versos libres*, however, was not published until 1913, in a Cuban edition that included *Ismaelillo* and *Versos sencillos*, which probably had a limited circulation.

Modernismo, chiefly Darío but also Martí, generated an overabundance of poets throughout Latin American and Spain. They were, mostly, aspiring Daríos, though some were original enough to become notable and gain access to the movement's mainstream, and each country seemed to have its own modest Modernista luminary. Another Cuban, Julián del Casal (1863–93), wrote remarkable poetry and prose during his very brief life, which he led in an even more decadent style than Darío, emulating the French *poètes maudits*, particularly Baudelaire (he yearned to go to Paris but only got as far as Madrid). His *Nieve* (Snow, 1892) and *Bustos y rimas* (Busts and Rhymes, 1893) contains poems of arresting beauty, some evoking paintings and statues in a cold atmosphere in which, by contrast with the Cuban climate, they seem to exist in an independent ambiance of their own. Casal's is a radically gloomy poetry, deep in its evocation of "the glacial country of madness," as he put it.

José Asunción Silva (1865–96), a Colombian who also died young, like Martí and Casal, was a follower of Poe and an experimenter who tried free verse and unusual metrical schemes. This he did, above all, in his superb "Nocturno," a poem filled with dark melancholy in which the short and long lines, with no discernible pattern in their rhythm, seem to evoke sobs, or stammering. Silva had the rare ability to utilize silences and pauses to create a somber beauty evocative of music. In spite of his limited production, he is one of the major Modernista poets.

Bello's modernity stemmed from his awareness of being the founder of a tradition, of an American poetic language, and even of an American Spanish, rooted in history but fresh and ready to reflect and articulate new realities. His multifarious, ambitious poetry sought to chart a new intellectual and political course, even if his verse was still tied to neoclassical conventions.

Darío's Modernismo came as a result of Latin America's immersion in the new scientific and industrial realities of the second half of the nineteenth century, when the nature that Bello sang about as being subjected to agriculture was being exploited by new, far-reaching techniques, and the traditional ways and customs of what had been colonial Latin America were being replaced by those created by the capitalist frenzy of Europe and the United States. The outcome of the Spanish-American War signaled this change. Darío's poetry, and that of his many followers, countered with the creation and contemplation of beauty, and with a spiritualism that opposed the profitable, the pragmatic, and the certain. In "Lo fatal" (What is Fatal), from the 1905 *Cantos de vida y esperanza*, Darío answered the confidence of positivism in science and self-assertion in business and politics with this very twentieth-century line: "To be, and to know nothing, to exist without a known bearing." He both deflated the certainties of modernity and opened the way to modernity.

Chapter 3
Nineteenth-century prose: the revelation of Latin America

The chronicles of the discovery and conquest, in spite of vigorous poetic activity in the viceroyalties, dominate the panorama of colonial letters by their sheer numbers, size, and influence. During the Enlightenment and through the nineteenth century, however, the writing that prevailed in Latin America was that of descriptive and analytic prose, even when it took the form of fiction as short stories or novels. Prose is more attuned than poetry to political developments, and because nations were in the process of being founded throughout the continent during the nineteenth century, political writing, including polemics about institutions, epistles, and even the drafting of constitutions and legal codes was a major endeavor; these kinds of writing influenced what is commonly thought of as literature.

Another kind of writing that influenced literature was that issuing from the emergent social sciences: sociology, criminology, and above all anthropology. These, in turn, were often modeled after the writings of the many European scientific travelers who crisscrossed the continent and who wrote voluminous and detailed books about the flora, fauna, geography, and demography of Latin America. Chief among these was Alexander von Humboldt, a figure of the foremost importance in the development of the new nations. Conventional generic distinctions are difficult to apply to nineteenth-century Latin American writing, where political manifesto, sociological tract, anthropological study, public oratory, essayistic writing, newspaper chronicle, and social sketch commingle.

Narrative, even fictional stories, implies history, a temporal unfolding, which in turn calls for beginnings: when did time, the time we inhabit, begin? In the colonial chronicles the "Discovery" was seen as the only major break in Western history since the birth of Christ. Such was the view propounded by Fray Bartolomé de las Casas, who also held that the Aztecs and Incas were akin to the Romans. This idea was repeated by Garcilaso de la Vega, el Inca, in his *Royal Commentaries*, where he said that Cuzco and Mexico City were indeed like Rome; the centers of great civilizations that lacked only Christianity to be on a par with Europe. By the nineteenth century, history had acquired a much deeper past, as scientists discovered and studied fossils that proved that time reached down to a bottomless origin from which the universe had evolved. New schemes had to be devised to write about the history of the Americas, particularly as independence provided a new political beginning.

It was one of Bello's pupils, none other than Simón Bolívar (Venezuela, 1783–1830), who was among the first to ponder the future of the nations that he brought into being in a text that stands at the gateway into Latin American meditations on the identity of its culture, known as "La carta de Jamaica" (The Letter from Jamaica, 1815). The Liberator had retired to Jamaica after a disagreement over the conduct of the siege of Santa Marta. There he wrote this letter, in the style of classical epistles, addressed to a "Gentleman of this Island," probably the British governor. This conceit allows him to write as if in dialogue with his correspondent, a cultured man to whom the situation and future of Latin America has to be explained from the ground up. In the letter he justifies the revolutionary war, declares himself against monarchies, federalism, and democracy, and outlines his project for the Republic of Colombia, which would unite Nueva Granada

(roughly today's Colombia) and Venezuela. His grandiose idea
is the creation of a large country, with its capital in the Isthmus
of Panama; in fact, given its advantageous position straddling
Atlantic and Pacific oceans, he wonders if it could not, eventually,
be the capital of the whole world.

Bolívar's range of allusions reveals his merging—like Bello—of a
neoclassical education with a Romantic penchant for the local.
He mentions or quotes Las Casas, von Humboldt, Rousseau,
Montesquieu, and Saint-Pierre, and considers the various kinds
of states proposed by the French Enlightenment thinkers. He
declares, however, that the forms of representative government
that they favor are not fit for countries that have just thrown off
the yoke of the Spanish Empire, whose ills he underlines in what
sound like echoes of the Black Legend. Bolívar's most often quoted
statement about the emerging Latin America is a call to heed its
difference and specificity in historical, geographical, and natural
terms:

> We are a small human race of our own. We possess a separate world,
> surrounded by vast seas; we are neophytes in nearly all the arts
> and sciences, although in a certain fashion very old in the ways of
> civil society. I look upon the present state of America like that of
> the Roman Empire when it was dismembered and each member
> created a political system according to its interests or following the
> particular interests of some of its leaders, families or corporations.
> But with one difference: those dispersed members went back to
> re-establish their ancient nations with the changes that new things
> and goals demanded, while we barely retain vestiges of what existed
> in the past, because we are neither Indian nor European, but an
> intermediate type made up of the legitimate proprietors of the land
> and the invading Spaniards.

Bolívar's conundrum will be the bane as well as the point of
departure for most modern Latin American literature: how to be
European in a different way, how to balance a European mind-set

and a Latin American context that escapes or even seems to be at odds with it, and how to express in writing these concerns.

The clash between civilization (Europe) and barbarism (America) will be at the core of the debate of Latin American literature and will first be articulated in those terms by Domingo Faustino Sarmiento who, like Bolívar, was not a detached observer but a very engaged participant in shaping his world. Others, namely José Martí and José Enrique Rodó, will continue the polemic, which permeated fiction and even poetry (as in Esteban Echeverría's "The Captive").

The wider issue of how to reveal the specificity of Latin American reality in writing will dominate Latin American literature from now on, aided by the turn to realism in fiction, which will call for descriptions as accurate and comprehensive as possible of the various geographical, cultural, and demographic contexts. The scientific travelers' writing, the methods of the emerging social sciences, and the rhetoric and techniques of realism in literature and the arts in general will provide the approach. A variety of realism called *costumbrismo* will prevail in Latin America precisely because its aim is to depict the customs of the folk, particularly those living in the marginal neighborhoods of cities.

Costumbrismo emerged from a combination of a Romantic interest in the common people, in nature in all its detail, and the conventions of realism, which had been developing since the work of Cervantes. The tendency favored brief, highly focused, descriptive texts that came to be known as *cuadros de costumbres* and in French *tableau des moeurs*; the development of newspapers encouraged this propensity. "Cuadro" and "tableau" reveal costumbrismo's kinship with painting, its effort to paint with words, as it were. "Costumbre" means custom, so costumbrismo concentrated on mores, habits, activities, often crafts and trades. These had to be appealing because of their oddity, hence the people depicted were peasants, workers, or people inhabiting poor

4. A statue of Simon Bolívar in Caracas, Venezuela.

neighborhoods in cities, so both the observer and intended reader belonged to an upper echelon of society, the bourgeoisie or higher.

The characters in costumbrista sketches were colorful, sometimes literally so (meaning that they were people of color), and their activities and the setting of their actions picturesque. Costumbrista writers paid close attention not just to the actions of the people but also to their clothing, tools, animals, and other objects proper to their world. Costumbrismo was like an inventory of the real, a kind of proto-ethnography.

Though not all Latin American prose of the nineteenth century was costumbrista, the movement's general tenets prevailed both in prose fiction and in expository texts about the new nations' social and physical features. In some of the most important works of the period it is difficult to separate prose fiction from costumbrista sketch, both in the case of short stories and longer genres. This is at the same time a virtue and a defect. Much Latin American fiction of the nineteenth century is overladen with description, a weakness that continues in the twentieth century; and many descriptive works are laced with a surfeit of anecdotes that are presumably appealing because of their colorfulness. The drive behind this descriptive tendency among Latin American writers is probably the feeling that because they felt themselves to be in that complicated and extraordinary situation of which Bolívar speaks, they must insistently explain it to their intended readers and to themselves.

Such a predicament led to the publication of what is considered the first Latin American novel, *El periquillo sarniento* (The Itching Parrot, 1816), by the Mexican José Joaquín Fernández de Lizardi (1776–1827), a prolific pamphleteer and minor poet. Lizardi found in the Spanish picaresque a perfect vehicle for his satirical picture of Mexican society. Cervantes's work and Mateo Alemán's *Guzmán de Alfarache* provided a realistic lens through which to narrate the life of a young, poor man who works for several masters, giving Lizardi the opportunity to offer a gallery of portraits besides that of the protagonist. Narrated in the first person, *El periquillo sarniento* provides a moralistic image of society and a critical life of the protagonist who, more than immoral, is weak and prone to follow bad influences. Thus his novel is moralistic and didactic, reflecting the teachings of Rousseau in the creation of his protagonist. It is a book that follows the ideas of the Enlightenment and, in that respect, is attuned to ideological currents that led to Mexican independence, though its author was not a proponent of it.

Much more successful examples of costumbrismo appeared in Argentina. The first was written by Esteban Echeverría (1805–51). Echeverría wrote in "El matadero" (The Slaughterhouse) one of the finest pieces of Latin American fiction of the nineteenth century. Written around 1838, it denounces the dictator Juan Manuel de Rosas, but it was unfortunately not published during Echeverría's lifetime. It is a fairly extensive, tautly written short story that narrates the brutal assassination by a bunch of thugs at the Buenos Aires slaughterhouse of a young man who opposes the dictator.

The costumbrista element is the detailed, gruesome description of the activities at the slaughterhouse and of the role the institution plays in the city's culture and economy. It is a brilliant sketch, perhaps the best piece of politically inspired fiction ever written in Latin America. But the story's power lies in the drama of the young man's slaying: because it mimics that of the slaughterhouse animals, it takes on the air of an atavistic ritual sacrifice. It is as if the slaughter were a scene of men re-enacting their subhuman origins while at the same time it becomes an allegory representing Argentina in the hands of Rosas and his henchmen.

Rosas's dictatorship would also inspire Domingo Faustino Sarmiento (Argentina, 1811–88) to write the most important book ever authored by a Latin American: *Civilización y barbarie: vida de Juan Facundo Quiroga* (The Life of Facundo Quiroga: Civilization and Barbarism, 1845). This is the work in which the dialectics or "civilization and barbarism" at the core of Latin American culture first expressed by Bolívar would be most thoroughly considered. *Facundo*, as the book is known, is a work combining various genres. It began as a political pamphlet, written against Rosas while Sarmiento was exiled in Chile. Sarmiento set out to write a biography of Facundo Quiroga, a provincial caudillo who had risen from gaucho to governor of La Rioja using the brutal methods with which his background had endowed him. The aim was to show that Rosas's dictatorship had its origin in the barbarism of the *pampas*, which had to be tamed with the civilization already prevailing in cultivated Buenos Aires, a capital that had modeled itself after the great European metropolises. Facundo would be like a specimen whose case study would reveal the barbaric essence that the Argentine character derived from the pampas' wilderness. This is the scientific thrust of Sarmiento's book, its presumed method.

But Sarmiento was a Romantic at odds with his rationalistic inclinations, which he had learned reading European books. *Facundo* turned out to be a wide-ranging, detailed, and loving description of the Argentine pampas and countryside in general.

Sarmiento pays close attention to gaucho culture in all its manifestations, from the gaucho's love of horses and horsemanship to his stoic aloofness and indifference to hardship and pain; from his unflinching courage to his astonishing skills with lasso and knife; from his minute knowledge of vast tracts of land and uncanny ability to orient himself in desertlike regions to his artistic tendencies as minstrel. Sarmiento chooses individual gauchos displaying each of those features and describes them in detail, telling riveting stories along the way.

There are unforgettable portraits of pathfinders, of *payadores* (minstrels), of *baqueanos* (guides), who know the pampas even by the taste of its various kinds of grass, of *rastreadores* (pathfinders), those who can follow the trails of fugitive men or animals (horses and cattle), minding the most subtle clues, and others who have developed a savage science derived from their environment and sufficient to cope with its challenges. This is ultimately what Sarmiento demonstrates in enthralling and excruciating detail: a gaucho society that has sprung up from the pampas and that is at one with it. In other words, Sarmiento loves what he presumably hates: barbarism.

5. A gathering of gauchos, ca. 1890–1923.

This struggle at the heart of *Facundo* is one of the elements of its literary appeal. Another is the portrayal of the protagonist. Sarmiento provides many anecdotes to show Quiroga's savagery, but in the end the caudillo emerges as a tragic figure, not only because he is betrayed by Rosas, who has him killed, but because Quiroga knows that he is going to be ambushed at Barranca Yaco and refuses to cancel his trip or deviate from his route. Like a tragic hero, Quiroga goes forth resolutely to meet his fate. This is the reason why he is legendary, and also the reason why he deserves to be the protagonist of Sarmiento's book. Sarmiento elevates the depiction of the life of the folk to high literature by showing that they are endowed with intelligence, competence, and courage, and that they have devised a full life, complete with all the features of civilization. Sarmiento, ultimately, does not take sides in the dichotomy laid out by Bolívar: he leaves it as what it is, a dialectic process out of which Argentine, and by extension Latin American, life is developing. He has also left a book that, for all the polemics it has created since its publication, cannot be bypassed and into whose compelling drama even its most acerbic critics are drawn.

Like Bolívar, Sarmiento was very much engaged in the development of the society in which he lived. He was an educator, like Bello, who did much to advance Argentine schooling and eventually became president of Argentina. (He and Bartolomé Mitre [1821–1906], another Argentine intellectual, poet, military officer, and translator of Horace and Dante, who also reached the presidency, began a Latin American tradition that extends to the present.) It was in that capacity that Sarmiento put into practice policies aimed at making Argentina as European as possible, policies that made him a polemical figure in the history of Latin America because he was associated with racialist conceptions of the new nations. But the struggle against Indians and the effort to modernize Argentina preceded Sarmiento and, whatever we think of them now, shaped the country as we know it today.

To see him as the proponent of civilization (European, whites) against barbarism (non-European, colored) is to caricaturize Sarmiento who maintained with pride that under the Argentine's European garb, a gaucho was concealed. In the Caribbean, the problems faced by Sarmiento had different protagonists; instead of gauchos and Indians, African slaves and their descendents created the conflicts involved in the establishment of new nations. The historical differences between the regions were major. The Africans were not in their land of origin, like the Indians and gauchos; their relative numbers were vast because of the labor demands of the sugar industry; and the emerging countries of the Caribbean were still under Spanish domination, not independent.

Still, the situation was structurally similar: it involved the assimilation of peoples whose cultures were radically different into civic societies based on Western ideas. In the case of the Africans, because of the distance from their homelands, the violent way they were wrested from them, and the variety of ethnic groups that they represented, their cultures had been destroyed and had to be rebuilt practically from the ground up and in unfamiliar circumstances. The harshness of sugar production, driven by a demanding international market, the development of machinery that accelerated the production process and imposed increasingly rigorous working conditions, and the struggles for independence from Spain by Creole groups, above all in Cuba, made for a very dramatic state of affairs.

Soon the aspirations for independence and the liberation of the slaves became common causes for intellectuals and artists as well as many others, and this coalescence gave rise to Cuban literature in the first half of the nineteenth century. As in Argentina and other regions of Latin America, costumbrismo was the underlying literary trend in prose, which soon acquired an antislavery thematic and made blacks and mulattoes the protagonists of more ambitious literary works, which included costumbrista sketches, and eventually full-fledged novels. The rebellious political and literary group, which was the counterpart of the Asociación de Mayo in Argentina, gathered in Havana at the home of Domingo del Monte, a Venezuelan-born writer and cultural promoter.

Romantics like the Argentines, these intellectuals found in the black slave a suitable pariah for their literary creations, and in the culture of blacks and mulattoes—some belonging to an emerging colored bourgeoisie—an attractive subject for their costumbrista sketches and novels. Among the writers was Anselmo Suárez y Romero (1818–78), who became known for his brief, descriptive sketches of life in the sugar mills, where slaves toiled in horrible conditions to which he called attention with such a keen eye for detail that one can see in them an emerging ethnography.

Suárez y Romero wrote an important novel, *Francisco o las delicias del campo* (Francisco or The Delights of the Countryside, written in 1838 but not published until 1880), which is a scathing denunciation of slavery. It narrates the unfortunate life of Francisco, a slave in the house of the widow Mendizábal in Havana. He falls in love with Dorotea, another house slave, who is desired by the widow's son, Ricardo, a cruel and frivolous womanizer. *Francisco* has a tightly woven plot, and its descriptions of life in the sugar mill, both that of the slaves and of their white owners, are sharp, detailed, and meaningful.

This is costumbrismo at its best, including the pointed political critique, which is on a par with Echeverría's "El matadero." Suárez y Romero's *Francisco* had been preceded by *Sab* (1841), with a similar theme and story, written by Gertrudis Gómez de Avellaneda (1814–73). Gómez de Avellaneda was a skillful novelist, whose other novel, *El artista barquero* (The Artist Boatman, 1861), a romance set in France about a young artist who tries to win his beloved by painting a convincing landscape of Cuba for her father, a Marseilles-based businessman who had fallen in love with the island while living there for commercial purposes. This novel is a much more valuable work of fiction than *Sab*, which has nevertheless attracted more attention because of its antislavery theme.

Neither Suárez y Romero nor Gómez de Avellaneda can measure up to Cirilo Villaverde (1812–94) and his *Cecilia Valdés o la Loma del Ángel* (*Cecilia Valdés or El Angel Hill*, 1882). Villaverde, who favored Cuban independence and lived as an exile in the United States for many years, devoted most of his life to writing *Cecilia Valdés*. *Cecilia Valdés* is an ambitious, substantial work of fiction whose protagonist, taken up in the twentieth century by musical theater, became a Cuban icon, a nationalist symbol of the island's people. The novel's conflicts spring from Cecilia's beauty. She is a very light-skinned mulatta courted by the rich, white, young man Leonardo Gamboa. The Cinderella plot lurks behind this predicament, but here it is much more complicated and leads to a very sad ending.

What neither Cecilia nor Leonardo knows is that they are half siblings. She is the illegitimate daughter of Don Cándido, Leonardo's Spanish father, the wealthy owner of a sugar mill and involved in other businesses, including the slave trade. Incest is at the core of *Cecilia Valdés*: one of Leonardo's full sisters, Adela, is the spitting image of Cecilia, and Leonardo lavishes attentions on her in a dubious way. Meanwhile, Leonardo's mother, Doña Rosa, is so taken with her son that she gives him gifts and money to indulge his passion for women: she does not really want him married. Leonardo is betrothed to Isabel Ilincheta, a white young woman of his social class, a relationship that he pursues lukewarmly while consummating his liaison with Cecilia. Cecilia is assiduously courted by Pimienta, a mulatto musician and tailor, who, knowing Cecilia's racial origins, feels more entitled to her than Leonardo. This conflict culminates at Leonardo's and Isabel's wedding, when Pimienta rushes up to the groom and stabs him to death. Cecilia has already given birth to Leonardo's child, a baby girl, and is in a hospital, suffering a severe nervous crisis.

Villaverde unfolds this plot while providing, as backdrop, a thick description of Cuban society at all levels, from the white, rich elite to the slaves in Havana and the sugar mills. In the Cuban capital, described in such minute detail that one can follow the action on a map of the city, there are lavish balls attended by the rich, colored dances attended by the emerging colored bourgeoisie (no slaves allowed), and scenes in the slums where the criminal elements engage in illegal and violent activities. The gallery of characters from the various social classes, drawn in superb satirical fashion, constitutes one of the great virtues of the novel. Villaverde has also cast all the conflicts among the characters in finely and authentically sketched political circumstances. The conflict among the Spaniards is noticeable, but less so than that between the Spaniards and the Creole Cubans, who yearn for independence from the mother country. The split between Don Cándido and his Cuban-born son Leonardo brilliantly dramatizes this political battle dividing the white elite.

The more pressing political crisis is fostered by slavery. Don Cándido imports slaves directly from Africa, sidestepping the ban on the practice imposed by a treaty between Spain and England. Slavery is legal in Cuba, however, and is the mainstay of the sugar industry. Many Cuban intellectuals, artists, and writers ardently opposed slavery, to which they added their desire for independence. This explosive conflict is at the heart of *Cecilia Valdés*. Erotic, social, and political conflicts coalesce in *Cecilia Valdés*, making the novel a masterpiece of nineteenth-century realism.

Other, more conventional and canonical nineteenth-century Latin American novels, like *Amalia* (1851–55), by the Argentine José Mármol (1817–71), and *María* (1867), by the Colombian Jorge Isaacs (1837–95), pale in comparison to *Cecilia Valdés*, but they are worthy works that have withstood the test of time. A third work, *Aves sin nido* (Birds Without Nests, 1889), by the Peruvian Clorinda Matto de Turner (1854–1909), perhaps because of its theme, which is parallel to that of *Cecilia Valdés*, is a more poignant novel that announces modern literary and ideological trends. Isaacs's *María* is, at first glance, an adaptation of Chateaubriand's *Atalá* to the real America that the French idealized. Efraín, in fact, reads to his beloved, María, pages of *Atalá*, which at times seems like the script they are following. *María* suffered from the saccharine love rhetoric of the protagonists, particularly Efraín, so distant from our contemporary sensibility. Matto de Turner's *Aves sin nido* narrates the story of Manuel and Margarita, lovers who turn out to be the children of the parish priest by two different Indian women.

A Peruvian prose writer who did successfully distort Peruvian reality, and one of the most important cultural figures of nineteenth-century Latin America, was Ricardo Palma (1872–1910). He is credited with having "invented" a genre with his *tradiciones*. These were brief, mildly satirical stories about colonial Peru. The country had such a rich colonial past (Lima was one of the most populous and sumptuous colonial viceregal capitals, the counterpart of Mexico City) that the historical and anecdotal archive was vast. Once Palma found his formula—quaint little stories about colorful people—he fell into a recognizable pattern of plot, character, and incident.

Because of his care for style and structure, Palma was instrumental in the development of the artistic short story in Latin America, and his incorporation of fantastic elements makes him a clear precursor of magical realism. The tradiciones were published in books from 1872 to 1891, after having appeared in newspapers. One collection, more than mildly pornographic, had the title *tradiciones en salsa verde* (tradiciones in green—i.e., smutty—sauce). Romantic in their evocation of the past, the tradiciones portray the colonial period as devoid of the social conflicts that actually characterized it. Through Palma's miniaturist art, Peru under Spanish rule seemed like a sometimes humorous world of legend and romance. Palma found a receptive audience in a post-independence Peruvian bourgeoisie that longed for an imagined history of privilege and pageant. Like Sarmiento, Mitre, and many Latin American authors to follow, Palma was multifaceted. He was a senator, a journalist, a playwright, and the author of historical volumes. He was also the founder and first director of Peru's national library.

Two essayists, José Martí (Cuba, 1853–95) and José Enrique Rodó (Uruguay, 1872–1917), close the founding century of modern Latin American literature, with contrasting views about the relationship of Latin America to Europe. Both had a tremendous impact on Latin American thought and literature. In spite of their radical differences, they have much in common, and their views are more complimentary than contradictory.

To begin with, both are part of the Modernista movement. Martí was one of the key figures of Modernista poetry. Rodó was probably the best prose writer of the movement. Both looked beyond their individual countries to engage the whole of Latin America in their consideration, being in that sense the heirs of Bolívar. In their analyses both Martí and Rodó are very much aware of the United States as political power and cultural influence. Martí lived for fifteen years in New York and was steeped in American literature and thought. Rodó wrote in the aftermath of the Spanish-American War, which Martí had been instrumental in starting by promoting the Cuban war of liberation to which he gave his life. To Bolívar the United States was a model to imitate in its separation from the metropolis; by the time Martí and Rodó wrote, the United States had become a leading imperial nation whose technical and industrial strength was made obvious by its easy defeat of the Spanish. Finally, both Martí and Rodó were in dialogue with Sarmiento, for whom the United States was an example to follow in many realms.

The genre in which Martí had no equal was oratory, and some of his best-known prose pieces began as speeches delivered to Cuban workers and veterans of the Ten Years War living in the United States. His speeches are charged with emotion, intended to rouse his audience to war. But he had a penchant for highly original, elaborate tropes in which the poet in Martí shows his talents. Martí's best poetry is contained in his speeches, which were also aphoristic, and from which strings of *pensamientos* (adages) have been culled and used for educational and doctrinal purposes.

Martí's newspaper chronicles and essays were, during his lifetime, his greatest literary success. These texts share much with costumbrismo, which is applied to life in the United States and in the other countries that he visited,: Mexico, Guatemala, and Venezuela. They are a blend of reportage, tableau, and essay that Martí took to its highest form through his powerful imagination, poetic eye, and ability to use striking tropes. He often wrote them not as an eyewitness report but from a collection of newspaper releases that he took from the wire or from American newspapers.

The chronicles found an eager audience because they dealt with—indeed were written from within—the United States, whose transformation into a major power inspired awe, admiration, fear, and, in some cases, resentment among Latin Americans. Martí was writing from within a country that dwarfed Europe in material progress and sheer physical size. In his chronicles, Martí captured the social, industrial, and political effervescence of the United States from the perspective of a Latin American who was both admiring and critical—detached from the events themselves, but not totally, for Martí was living in the United States and profiting from the opportunities and freedoms that the country offered to launch the liberation of his own. This mix, together with Martí's captivating style, was irresistible to his public, and the volume of Martí's publications attests to the recognition he enjoyed among newspaper editors in Latin America.

When he wrote about Latin America, which was often and incisively, Martí had the advantage of knowing the history of its developing nations and being aware of the political traps into which they had fallen. He was most critical of the rise of ruling elites who were oblivious to the plight of the poor, particularly the Indian masses, which he was able to observe in Mexico and Central America. Martí was also wary of the dangerous escalation of militarism, of the growth of a ruling class of military men and their descendents who had attained power during and after the wars of independence. Martí feared the turn to militarism among the former leaders of the Ten Years War who he was trying to organize to start a new war of liberation in Cuba.

Militarism had already created rifts among them, and it would continue to haunt the independence movement. Of Martí's concerns about the future of Cuba, militarism was the most justified and the one that unfortunately became a nightmarish reality in the nation after independence. But Martí had both hope and confidence in the future of Latin America if it followed its own character, built upon the New World's bountiful and varied nature.

Martí's best-known essay on this topic is the aptly titled "Nuestra America" (Our America), published in a Mexican newspaper in 1891. An inspired, rousing essay calling for a Latin American approach to understand and govern Latin America, Martí counters Sarmiento's arguments in favor of European civilization, while at the same time arguing for the sort of intimate knowledge of Latin American reality that Sarmiento both espoused and practiced in his *Facundo*. Martí writes, contradictorily echoing Rousseau, "There is no clash between civilization and barbarism, but between false erudition and nature. Natural man is good, and accepts and rewards superior intelligence, as long as the latter does not take advantage of his subjection to harm him."

Martí's nationalist plea has found many followers in Latin America, aided no doubt by his self-immolation in the field of battle, which has set the bar very high for would-be revolutionaries. His arguments, contradictory as they are in many respects, are really a synthesis of what Bolívar and even Sarmiento had been arguing for, and do not, as they appear at first glance, pre-empt or disagree with those of Rodó, made only a few years later.

Rodó's "Ariel" (1900) is the most influential Latin American essay ever published. Its title is that of the character in Shakespeare's *The Tempest*, a sprite or airy spirit, a statue of whom graces the room in which an old professor, known as Prospero, from the same play, addresses his students on the last day of class. The essay is a critique of positivism, pragmatism, and the mechanical conception of life allied to material, industrial progress, incarnate in the United States, whose easy defeat of Spain in the just concluded (1898) Spanish-American War alarmed Rodó. He was not so much troubled by the United States' imperial policies as with its influential materialistic culture, which was being admired and imitated throughout Latin America.

Rodó is an acerbic critic of the American Way of Life so much admired by Sarmiento. Rodó's Latin Americanism is not like Martí's, based on the specificity of Latin American nature or racial composition, as it is on its European, chiefly Latin (in the sense of Roman-derived) culture. He conceives this culture to be spiritual, artistic, idealistic, opposed to the crass materialism and commercialism of the United States. Rodó considers such a culture superior, more worthy of cultivation and imitation than that coming from the north. Rodó struck a chord in the Latin American psyche, one attuned to cultural origins but also motivated by frustration, resentment, and even envy.

The picture of the United States that appears in "Ariel" is a distortion, almost a caricature. American culture was not oblivious to artistic values, not just in its thriving literature, which included major poets like Whitman and Poe, and thinkers like Emerson, but in everyday life. To realize this one only has to think of the magnificent railroad stations being built at the end of the nineteenth century throughout the United States, which were like modern cathedrals in their adaptation of architectural beauty to modern technological needs. But Rodó needed the example of the United States for emphasis. His quarrel was against positivistic philosophy; it was a war of ideas, not of ideology. Unlike Martí, he had no real experience of the United States and did not live in an area that was threatened by its military might. Yet his appeal to European values was an instant success. His book circulated rapidly throughout Latin America, where Ariel "clubs" were even founded to discuss it. Rodó became a celebrity on the heels of Darío, whom he greatly admired.

Rodó's is a splendid prose. In contrast to Martí's it is cool, measured, with expansive cadences and sustained metaphors. Rodó sometimes invents stories to make his points. In "Ariel," to describe the life of the spirit, he imagines an elaborate castle in which an elderly king keeps himself away from the noise and bustle of the outer world. It is a fine fable of an enclosure within an enclosure, that of the make-believe classroom in which the old professor delivers his valedictory oration. It is not without dissonant tropes, such as those used to describe the process by which ideas are imprinted in the soul of the listeners, in which there lurk violent actions, such as that of striking coins to imprint figures in them. Rodó's is a full literary discourse that includes a jarring clash of concepts and images in a vain but stubborn search for full expression. There is an implicit, conflictive self in the voice of Prospero, the emblem of which is the heavy statue of Ariel whose meaning is presumed to be spiritual and weightless. It is in this deep stratum that "Ariel" conceals a kind of subconscious of modern Latin American writing, one in which that "most extraordinary and complicated situation" in which Bolívar says Latin Americans find themselves is always trying to find a solution.

Chapter 4
Poetry from Modernismo to Modernism

The biggest challenge facing Latin American poets in the wake of Modernismo was how to overcome Darío's influence. On a deep level it was impossible. Darío created a poetic stance, a voice, and an idiom for Spanish poetry that endure to the present. But poets had to shed his manner, and even that was not easy. Darío's poetry, disseminated widely because of the increasing proliferation of newspapers and magazines, permeated all poetry in Spanish, even popular songs. But ambitious poets, in search of originality and novelty had to find new ways to express themselves. Eventually, the avant-garde movements of the 1920s, what in English is called Modernism, provided a fresh poetics, one that, by discarding traditional prosody, led to the difficult kind of poetry that is still with us.

What Darío had done, particularly in his later poetry, like that in *Cantos de vida y esperanza*, was to acclimate the advances of symbolism to Spanish, something that had not been accomplished on either side of the Atlantic. This meant, above all, that poetry was not just the expression of individual feeling and a reflection of nature, like that of the Romantics, or the composition of exquisite verses, like that of the Parnassians, but a combination of both to achieve a kind of beauty that was the deep manifestation of poetic language rigorously subjected to the search for truth, for the absolute. Not even the best peninsular poets of the nineteenth century, like Gustavo Adolfo Bécquer, had reached that level, and among Darío's cohorts in Latin America, Martí, Silva, and Casal did so only sporadically.

The decadent lifestyle and the priestly devotion to poetry, disregarding all else, were an ancillary but significant part of that quest. This was the Romantic legacy. But the unrelenting search for the ultimate fusion of beauty and truth in a poetic language devoid of sentimentality and resolutely rejecting everyday speech was only comparable to the coeval impressionist movement in painting. Some young Latin American poets inherited Darío's mantle, acquiring a following throughout the continent and, like Darío, began to be recognized in Spain, where poetry was never the same after him.

They were all the heirs of symbolism, which had been the self-conscious assertion of a modern poetic practice that has lasted. In France, where the movement began and from where it spread, it meant first of all a loosening up of the tight prosodic strictures of French, beginning with the mandatory use of Alexandrine verses and the adherence to prescribed rhyming and rhythmic patterns. The situation was different in Spanish (and it had been discarded in English long ago), because varieties of meter and rhymes were commonly accepted. But there was a poetic idiom in the language that fluctuated from the academic to the mannered traditional (phony popular), and in which a vast number of clichés and prosodic commonplaces had accumulated. Darío did away with all that using a wide array of stanzas, meters, and rhyme schemes, even inventing some.

The symbolists had eschewed prosodic rules. They followed only one: the intimate emotion of the poet determines the stops and the length of the line, which does not end in a rhyme, or does at best in an assonant rhyme. Or, if the rhyme is preserved, its role is now to trace a melodic motif and to punctuate throughout the poem the ending of the irregular lines that make it up. This was so particularly in Verlaine, for whom musicality was foremost. Mallarmé had been the other master of the symbolists; like him they maintained that the material world was nothing but appearances, symbols. But symbolizing what? Above all, they were symbols of the deep conditions that determined the appearances themselves. The most evanescent nuances were called upon to express the secret laws of nature and of being, of the self. Between the fluidity of appearances and the infinity of causes the particular reality of the body seemed to vanish. The whole of nature was nothing more than a dynamic image, a veiled and fluid symbol of eternal laws.

At a higher level of complication, this dematerialized world could also translate the sentimental state of the poet, or an idea. The sentiment hearkened back to Verlaine; the idea to Mallarmé. This program Darío's followers learned from him and directly from the French sources, as he had. It remained the basic poetic policy for those who tried to overcome him and for Latin American poetry for the balance of the twentieth century.

Two Mexicans are among the important poets that stand out during Darío's last years and beyond, Amado Nervo and Enrique González Martínez. Nervo (1870–1919) was greatly admired in his day and continues to appear in anthologies and programs of study throughout Latin America. He was a mystic, obsessed with God, interested in Oriental religions, and a reader of Nietzsche. Nervo proclaimed that he was satisfied with his fate and the world: "Cry? Why?" He wrote a poem to Kempis, "that pale ascetic," known by heart by many, but he is mostly remembered for "La amada inmóvil" (The Still Beloved), where he pours his heart out for his dead lover but remains optimistic in spite of his despair. Apolitical, Nervo was interested in erotic themes, with which he dealt prudishly. His poetry tends to be simple, prosaic, without the musicality of conventional Modernismo, yet he claimed that, inspired by his beloved "My poetry found arcane cadences." Nervo's placidly pathetic poetic persona, his search for God and fulfillment through love, found many devoted readers, and his fame at one point rivaled that of Darío. He was the first notable modern Mexican poet.

His compatriot, Enrique González Martínez (1871–1952), was probably a better poet, yet he is mostly remembered today for a poem whose anti-Darío resonances he did not mean. The poem's most celebrated line goes: "Twist the swan's neck, with its deceptive plumage." The swan, notoriously, was the symbol Darío chose for his poetry, both for its beauty and the question mark suggested by his curved neck. The line, and González Martínez's avowed preference for the owl, symbol of reason and wisdom, turned him into Darío's slayer and his poetry into the signpost for the end of Modernismo. But González Martínez was an admirer of the Nicaraguan, particularly of his later poetry. He also followed the themes of French symbolism. González Martínez was drawn by deep, final questions. His eyes, his pupils, read the dark book of night, as he put it. In a poem he meets a ghost, a man who was returning from death but does not find the right questions to ask him. In another poem, included in the appropriately titled collection *Los senderos ocultos* (The Hidden Paths, 1915), a character is a "romero," a pilgrim—etymologically someone traveling to Rome, meaning looking for the truth. There is music in his verse, and alliterations such as "Your pupils pregnant with problems," as well as highly original tropes, like "Deep life's crystal soul."

As in Mexico, Modernismo was the rage in the countries of the Southern Cone (Argentina, Uruguay, Paraguay), especially in the thriving metropolis of Buenos Aires, where Darío arrived in 1893 and became a celebrity. Many were the Nicaraguan's followers, but none were more accomplished than Leopoldo Lugones (Argentina, 1874–1938), who dominated Argentina's literary scene for thirty years, even being named inspector general of education, and eventually director of the national library. Lugones was not only a skillful, exquisite poet with superb control of all poetic resources but also an influential essayist and fiction writer. As an essayist he proposed in his collection of lectures, *El payador* (The Minstrel, 1916) that *El gaucho Martín Fierro* was the epic of Argentine identity, which unleashed a long polemic. His involvement in politics led him gradually to an ardent nationalism and to support authoritarian military governments.

Lugones was repudiated for this by some, but his literary accomplishments were such that he was recognized as a key figure by subsequent Argentine writers like Jorge Luis Borges, and Lugones remains a major figure in the history of Latin American poetry. Perhaps anguished by his political decisions and by an unfortunate love affair with a young woman, Lugones poisoned himself in 1938.

Lugones's first book of poems, *Las montañas de oro* (Golden Mountains, 1897), put him on the far side of Modernismo, that is, he exaggerated some of the novelties brought about by Darío and his disciples. His next book, *Los crepúsculos del jardín* (Garden Twilights, 1905) saw him perfect the Parnassian side of Modernismo and the symbolist penchant for stringing images, some of which were shockingly fresh, as when he writes "On the clothes hanger on the wall / the crucified tail coat." Or the following stanza from a moving poem called "El solterón" (The Bachelor):

> Through the pink clouds,
> the swallows, hunting
> invisible butterflies,
> trace mysterious letters
> as if penning goodbyes.

There is a tinge of Darío in this scene, with its rosy clouds, swallows, and butterflies, but to turn the darting of the swallows into writing, and writing into a farewell is novel; the trope strains Modernista metaphor. The key to the image is that the butterflies are invisible, making the swallows' flight gratuitous, free, like poetry, most relevant when what they do is writing. The goodbye adds a tinge of melancholy. Lugones was a very refined poet.

But his most significant book was *Lunario sentimental* (1909), a title that literally means "sentimental moon calendar." Lugones had come under the influence not only of the usual symbolists but of Jules Laforgue, which gave his poetry an ironic touch that moved it beyond Modernismo and announced the poets of the avant-garde or Modernism. The irony can already be felt in the title. Lugones has taken the moon of Romantic poetry, with its somber moods, and that of Modernismo, with its silvery rays highlighting the shapes of beautiful objects, and reduced it to a calendrical instrument. This is the moon of tides and other natural cycles, boringly predictable in its mutations. "Lunario" is not a pretty word in Spanish; it sounds vulgar. Lugones is introducing a note of common speech into poetry, something alien to Modernismo, which would not enter poetry until the avant-garde generation. To add "sentimental" to the title intensifies the irony, because excessive feelings are being spent on something as humdrum as a calendar. "Sentimental" adds a touch of kitsch to the title of the book. Lugones's wit is subtle, as is his humor, an element missing altogether from Modernista poetry. His novel stance and manner were recognized all over the Hispanic world, and he became a luminary in the horizon of Spanish-language poetry.

A different fate was that of Lugones's near contemporary and neighbor from nearby Montevideo, Julio Herrera y Reissig (Uruguay, 1875–1910), who never traveled, except across the River Plate to Buenos Aires. Though he had a coterie of friends and admirers during his short lifetime, his fame, which grew to be considerable and enduring, arrived posthumously. From a distinguished but impoverished family, Julio, as he was known, made the tower on top of his parents' house, which was essentially the upstairs of a notorious brothel in Montevideo, his study and literary salon. The structure gave the name to one of his most celebrated suite of poems, *La Torre de las Esfinges* (The Sphinxes' Tower, 1909).

Diagnosed with a heart condition in childhood, Julio used morphine and lived the life of a recluse and an addictive reader. He devoured the French symbolists in books brought to him from Paris by a friend. He also learned Latin and Greek, so his mythological allusions, though following the Modernista vogue, came from their original sources, and his pastoral excursus had a genuine classical foundation, as one can tell by his epigraphs. Herrera y Reissig's poems were published in Montevideo as *Los peregrinos de piedra* (The Stone Pilgrims) in 1910, but a subsequent Parisian edition of 1913, with a splendid prologue by the Venezuelan Rufino Blanco Fombona, is the book that circulated throughout Latin America and spread his fame.

Herrera y Reissig is known primarily for having pushed Modernismo farther than Lugones and also for having anticipated, with his proclivity for daring and multiple metaphors, the Dadaists and Surrealists. In addition, he bared his subconscious through grotesque figures and incorporated elements of occultism. Aware of his drug use, some critics, perhaps too literally, attribute to that the morbid aspects of his work. Yet his poetry has an unrestrained quality that one would never associate with Darío, or even Lugones. The avant-garde poets found a kindred spirit in Herrera y Reissig. He had already arrived to where they were going.

Darío was still alive and active when Herrera y Reissig wrote, but the movement he had created had clearly gone beyond him. The next group of significant poets, straddling Modernismo and the avant-garde, would be made up of four women, all from South America; three from the Southern Cone. That they were women was not in itself a novelty. The Cuban Gertrudis de Avellaneda had been one of the notable Latin American poets of the nineteenth century, and there were Modernista women poets, such as Juana

Borrero (1877–96), also a Cuban. But as women they signaled the strong foothold that poetry had gained in Latin American society with the advent of Modernismo and the wide public acclaim Darío had received. The fact that one of the women, Gabriela Mistral, was awarded the Nobel Prize also meant that Latin American literature, independent of Spanish literature, was beginning to be recognized in the West.

More important, these women brought to the new poetry a new slant and themes. Love and desire now appeared from a female perspective, with different symbols, subject to different constraints, and with a different approach to death. Physical beauty and decay were topics that now surfaced too. Motherhood and the love of children also enter poetry, in some cases in the form of lullabies. Resentment and complaint of male privileges turn up too, giving poetry a political tone that it currently lacked for the most part and anticipating the literature to come in the 1920s. These women were serious, committed poets who pursued final questions.

Darío met Delmira Agustini (Uruguay, 1886–1914) in Buenos Aires and was enthralled by her poetry, beauty, and charm. He wrote a prologue for her book *Los cálices vacíos* (The Empty Chalices, 1913) in which he said, memorably and accurately, that not since Saint Theresa had there been poetry of such intensity in Spanish. Delmira was mesmerized by the great man, whose poetry she so admired. A precocious, passionate young woman, she wrote poetry of as unabashed eroticism as was possible at the time and even went beyond, which brought her some grief. No Modernista poet, except for the scandalously gay Colombian Porfirio Barba Jacob (Miguel Ángel Osorio) (1880–1942), had published such explicitly sexual poetry. She shocked the bourgeois society in which she lived in provincial Montevideo, where she had been born and raised.

A friend of Herrera y Reissig and his group, she availed herself of the same French books they studied and emulated. From the symbolists she learned a metrical freedom that gave her poetry very startling and pleasing cadences that seek to match her sensuous themes. They are verses moved by passion and express it not just in the images and tropes but in their rhythms. There is no vulgarity in Agustini's elevated eroticism. She was a superb poet. In her own life, however, she experienced a more turbulent kind of sexuality. She ended her marriage after a month but later took on her former husband as a lover. During a clandestine encounter he murdered her and committed suicide.

Another Uruguayan poet, Juana de Ibarbourou (Juanita Fernández Morales) (1895–1979), lived a long life and enjoyed wide recognition, being called "Juana de América." Also a poet driven by desire, Ibarbourou was keenly aware of her body, of its beauty, of its palpitating cravings, and of potential decay. Hers was a pagan, joyful kind of eros, apparently devoid of Judeo-Christian guilt, which expanded to encompass nature in pantheistic rapture. She had captured that side of Modernista poetry: the exaltation of physical beauty for its own sake, or for the sake of pleasure. Her joy of the flesh extended to life after death, for she believed that her body would go on desiring and actually rise again. So in a poem she asks her lover to bury her in a very shallow grave, so that her flesh may feel the throb of life and be resurrected. She was as unabashed in her sexuality as Agustini: "Take me right now while it is still early / and I have fresh dahlias in my hand." Toward the end of her life Ibarbouru ruefully contemplated her deteriorating body, claiming that she was now "shadows," feeling nothing anymore "In the stopped-up hub of the petals." Her renown beyond the Southern Cone was large and lasted throughout most of her life, though by the end she was forgotten and cast aside. But she retains a solid place in Latin American literary history.

Alfonsina Storni (Argentina, 1892–1938) was also a passionate lover, but she was tortured by her sense of woman's subservience to man. Her early poetry manifests these contradictory feelings, which eventually led to her suicide. She was very successful at first, being the first woman to break into the male-dominated Buenos Aires literary cafe life. Her poetry, like her, was bold, fresh in every sense. She expressed both a pagan need for sensual love and contempt for men that bordered on revulsion. In her best-known poem she talks about how neither her father nor grandfather ever cried, being men of steel, but how her lover's tear fell into her mouth, and she had never tasted such poison in her life. She is a "weak woman," but one who understands, not in the sense of empathy, but of having the capacity to glean, to grasp tasting that tear the "Centuries of pain of which I learned as I drank it." By the end of her short life she turned her back on her fame and, abandoning the kind of poetry that had brought it to her, began to write hermetic, deeply troubled verse, including a truly remarkable sonnet, "I am going to sleep" in which she announces her intention to commit suicide. In October of 1938 she walked into the sea and drowned herself.

It is said that Gabriela Mistral (Lucila Godoy Alcayaga, Chile, 1889–1957) made up her melodious pen name, combining those of two of her favorite writers, Gabriele d'Annunzio and Frédéric Mistral, though the second part may have come from the *Mistral* wind of Mediterranean France. She was born in Vicuña, a provincial town, into a poor family of Basque and Indian background. Self-taught, she became a school teacher by age fifteen. Education would become an important part of her poetic persona, as she rose to become the poet with the largest following in Latin America and a world-renowned personality who played an important role in the educational systems of Mexico and Chile. She was Chilean consul in Naples, Madrid, and Lisbon, and lived the last years of her life in the United States. Mistral led campaigns in support of children who were victims of poverty and war, and wrote immensely popular lullabies that were sung by mothers all over the Hispanic world. Her fame both as a poet and as an ambassador for noble causes earned her the Nobel Prize for literature in 1945.

Mistral's life story is inseparable from her aura and implicated in the understanding of her poetry. Her first love shot himself, a trauma that marked her for the rest of her life; it inspired her first book of poems, *Sonetos de la muerte* (Death Sonnets, 1914), which won a provincial literary prize and brought her attention in Chile. Another volume, *Desolación* (Desolation), was published in New York in Spanish in 1922 and brought her a measure of international fame. In 1924 *Ternura* (Tenderness) appeared; it was a book whose theme was childhood, a subject that expanded to include motherhood in *Tala* (Felling), published in 1938 in Buenos Aires. These were her best poems. Mistral was by then widely recognized as a major voice in Spanish-language poetry and had assumed the role of itinerant celebrity poet that had earlier been played by Darío, and which would be picked up by Pablo Neruda and Octavio Paz in the future.

The suicide of her boyfriend fixated forever in Mistral's mind a sense of discontinuity with creation as proclaimed by the Christian doctrine, and she was a believer. It was this feeling that impelled her to talk to God in her poems. In one, memorably, she asks forgiveness for her dead lover, a plea for his inclusion among the blessed in spite of the mortal sin he had committed by killing himself. From her earliest poems Mistral was a serious though not somber poet. In her early poems she addresses not only God but also her dead beloved, whom she tries to console by telling him that she will go down into the grave to "dream" with him. In others she turns him into a child who needs cuddling, affection, and understanding. Mistral believed in the power of poetry as a form of lay prayer. Some of her poems have biblical themes and characters, like Ruth, with whom she identified. The tenderness for children she expressed was determined both by her frustrated maternity—she condemned herself to barrenness in protest for the disappearance of her beloved—and by the belief that they could repair the rupture caused by death. Her poems to and for children combine maternal tenderness with a cosmic aspiration for wholeness, as in this stanza from a lullaby:

God the Father silently rocks
his thousand worlds.
I feel his hand in the darkness
and rock my baby.

This was Mistral's triumph, to express pain and hope in ways
with which everyone could identify, in a poetry that made no
concessions to pathos and observed the highest standards of poetic
expression. For this she was respected and even revered.

Although Mistral's work continued to appear until the fifties, her
first book of poetry was published in 1914, the year that World War
I broke out and finally brought the nineteenth century to an end.
The kind of poetic wholeness in which the symbolists ultimately
believed, one that could be found in the depths of the poetic self
and its relation to the deep causes of the world of appearances
expressed in symbols, was shattered by the Great War, one that
pitted the great imperial powers of the nineteenth century against
each other. Europe was devastated, and with it the high promises
of the West became empty and lost their promise of a better future
for humanity.

Harbingers of the twentieth century had begun to appear in
the philosophy of Nietzsche, the work of Freud, and, in 1906,
Einstein's theory of relativity, all of which undermined common
perceptions of the psyche and of reality. Impressionism had
already shaken our expectations about the appearance of everyday
things and events, even the transparency of air and the effects
of light on our eyes. Since the turn of the century, new artistic
movements had been developing a worldview in which the
"correspondences" that Baudelaire had sung about were no longer
available.

Latin American poets could not readily find in European poetry
anymore a foundation on which to build their works; a radically
new idiom had to bc invented. The same feeling of loss as well as

of freedom, of course, was felt by the European artists themselves, who sought in avant-garde movements as extreme as Dadaism, Futurism, and Surrealism venues to express the new freedom. The avant-garde Latin American poetry, which reflected this state of affairs, found its first leaders in two Chileans, Vicente Huidobro and Pablo Neruda, and a context provided by a constellation of Spanish poets of the highest quality, which came to be known as The Generation of 27: Federico García Lorca, Vicente Aleixandre, Jorge Guillén, Rafael Alberti, Pedro Salinas, and Dámaso Alonso.

Two other Spanish poets from an earlier generation, Juan Ramón Jiménez, who would win a Nobel Prize in 1956, and Antonio Machado were active and influential. The combined work of all those poets and the new Latin American poetry, which would eventually comprise, beyond Huidobro and Neruda, César Vallejo, Jorge Luis Borges, Octavio Paz, Nicanor Parra, and José Lezama Lima, added up to a golden age of Spanish-language poetry.

If World War I was literally a worldwide cataclysmic event, two others shook the Hispanic nations, fostering a sense of shared ideals and a common idiom among poets from all of Latin American and Spain: the Mexican Revolution (1911–17) and the Spanish Civil War (1936–39). The latter, in particular, turned into an integrative process, a magnet for poets not only from the Spanish-speaking world but also from everywhere and from many languages. It was a defining moment for twentieth-century literature, but particularly for poets, who found themselves united by political causes, together in the streets of Madrid and Barcelona, and even on the field of battle. Among the Latin Americans there were Neruda, Vallejo, Nicolás Guillén, Paz, and many others of lesser fame. The Spanish Civil War brought together the artistic and political avant-garde movements for one incandescent moment, which was brief but had lasting consequences.

Avant-garde poetry took the symbolist drive to freedom to its highest peak, following the lead of precursors such as Lautréamont and Mallarmé. It not only abandoned prosodic conventions of meter, rhyme, and stanza but also grammatical and logical rules and principles. This move was parallel to Cubist, Dadaist, and Surrealist avoidance of realist practices in painting, the breaking up of space and the rejection of perspective as well as the use of colors in imitation of those in nature. Meaning in poetry was now dependent on images and metaphors with no obvious sequence linking them. Tropes represented states of mind freely associated, or associated following nonconventional practices, leaving it up to the reader to assemble them according to his or her own perceptions and state of mind. By most common standards much of modernist poetry is hermetic, inaccessible to the average reader with normal expectations. The breaks, the stops are arbitrary, sometimes reproduced visually on the page by unusual printing schemes, like the lines in a Cubist painting. Parallel developments occurred in narrative, and in other arts such as film (with montage, for instance). By the 1920s the new poets that emerged were heirs of Darío only in the most general and abstract way, but they did not begin, as Herrera y Reissig or Mistral, as Modernistas; they were full-fledged Modernists.

César Vallejo (1892–1938) was born in Santiago de Chuco, a small town in the Andes of northern Peru. Both his grandfathers were Spanish priests; both his grandmothers, their native concubines. Vallejo would always profess pained pride in his Indian background, and not a few echoes of Quechua slip into his poems. He went through secondary education in the provinces and twice started university studies only to drop out for lack of funds. Eventually he finished a bachelor's degree in philosophy and letters in 1915 at Trujillo. In subsequent years he studied law, also at Trujillo. In 1918 Vallejo published his first collection of verse, *Los heraldos negros* (Black Heralds), which brought him some attention, and he was able to secure jobs teaching and writing for newspapers. Now in Lima, Vallejo joined the artistic and intellectual avant-garde, which was turning to politics as the economic and social situation of Peru worsened. By 1923, after a political incident that landed him briefly in jail, Vallejo left for Paris, where he became a political activist and joined the Communist Party in 1931. This was followed by the obligatory trips to the Soviet Union and long periods of political work in war-torn Spain. Vallejo would never return home, but he carried Peru within him.

Los heraldos negros is a book written still under the sway of Modernismo, not so much Darío's as that of Lugones's *Lunario sentimental* (1909). It is a turning point in Latin American poetry, the beginning of Modernist as opposed to Modernista poetry, since Vallejo broke with syntactical and prosodic conventions, making his verse difficult to read. Poetry would no longer be of the kind that even the late Darío wrote, deep and somber but comprehensible to all. Vallejo's despair now expressed itself through tortured grammar and shocking figures; it was irrational and unwilling to be subjected to prosody. There are Parnassian vestiges of the early Darío that had infused all Latin American writing, but *Los heraldos negros* shares with Modernist poetry elsewhere an apocalyptic hopelessness characteristic of the first post–world war period—it is evident in the very title of the book. Something at the core of Western civilization had broken down, as T. S. Eliot expressed in *The Wasteland*, and art had to reflect such a breakdown, not cover it with a veil of beauty. The first lines of *Los heraldos negros*, which have become a commonplace in the Spanish language to express gloom, set the tone:

> One suffers such harsh blows in life . . . I can't tell!
> Blows like God's hatred; blows so hard it is
> as if the dregs of all suffering
> pooled within the soul . . . I can't tell.

Anguish, however, is not just pervasive and vague, as in those lines, it is also personal, contingent: grief for the death of a brother, for instance, or for that of a beloved. The beauty of despair in Vallejo's poetry is its intimacy but also its fervor and intensity, a sense of having been betrayed by God and all the useless religious rituals and prayers.

Though *Los heraldos negros* is a harbinger of things to come, Vallejo's next book, *Trilce* (1922), is so radical that it can hardly be said to have been announced by anything that he or anyone else had published before. It is the Latin American avant-garde book of poems par excellence, the benchmark of modern poetry in the language. Its very title is already an indication of its wildly inventive poetics: "trilce" is a made-up word whose root and meaning critics have been debating since the book's publication. It is as if Vallejo were saying that he is creating not just poetry but language itself. The poems that follow do justice to that bold beginning. *Trilce* combines breathtakingly innovative poetic discourse with ordinary everyday language. Syntax and spelling are deliberately flouted, making meaning difficult to fathom, even irrecoverable. Nothing like it had been written before in Spanish. *Trilce* was a catharsis that merged with the convulsion brought about by Vallejo's political awakening; he did not publish another book of poems again. His best was to come posthumously, in *Poemas humanos* (Human Poems), a book whose title was not his but his widow's, and is perhaps the best collection of poetry in modern Spanish poetry, rivaling Lorca's, Neruda's and Paz's.

In this book, which contains poems from the 1920s up to Vallejo's death and includes those written during the Spanish Civil War, the poetry often glides off into prose, tense and dense poetic prose, but prose. It is as if Vallejo were wont to remake poetry from everyday language about everyday things and chose to eschew prosody, or reach it only after having gone through prose and the prosaic. The poems are about ordinary lives, including his own, commonplace settings and situations that nonetheless contain transcendental messages concerning suffering, time, the banality of existence, the randomness of evil and sorrow, the commonality of human misery. I suppose this is the reason for the title (even if it is not Vallejo's), which opposes "human" to "divine," worldly to heavenly. The book includes within it a book dedicated to the defenders of the Spanish Republic at the front, where it was printed in 1938 but never bound, *España, aparta de mí este cáliz* (Spain, Take Away This Chalice).

España, aparta de mí este cáliz contains the most powerful, poignant, beautiful political poetry in the Spanish language. It evokes the artistic masterpiece of the war, Picasso's *Guernica*. It has the same apocalyptic force of the picture, a cry so loud against violence that it transcends partisanship. The tone is appropriately prophetic, with distinct echoes from the book of Revelation (the title, however, is from Matthew 36:29), with expressions of increasing emotion conveyed by escalating anaphora and a meaning that emerges through the accretion of figures of amazing originality. Some poems are new versions of common prayers, like the "Our Father." The book reflects the concluding moments of the war, when the defeat of the Republic was hanging on every battle, an enumeration of which gives the sequence of poems a narrative thread of sorts. No one has better expressed the clash of metal against flesh, or more movingly the death of ordinary men, particularly peasants, whose understanding of the conflict is more telluric than intellectual, and who enter death stoically. But Vallejo goes farther than human conflict and suffering. In his poems there is a generalized battle among things animate and inanimate, a whirling of matter in a state of chaos that is simply dazzling. He succumbed, like Byron, to the role of romantic victim of his vocation. On April 15, 1938, Good Friday, practically destitute, Vallejo died in Paris, the desired place for such a sacrifice by a Latin American poet, after years of poverty, despair, family and amorous disasters, and wearying political activism.

A more fortunate Latin American poet who lived for several years in Paris was the Chilean Vicente Huidobro (1893–1948), who was not on the level of the Peruvian but incarnated the avant-garde spirit as no other. His real surnames were García and Fernández, which could not be more ordinary, so he made up

Huidobro, showing from the start his fascination with words and fondness for breaking them up and putting them back together in unusual combinations. His attraction to French poetry was such that he turned into a French poet, publishing French poems in *Nord-Sud*, a Paris-based avant-garde journal published by Pierre Revérdy. Huidobro, who was quite adept at self-promotion, moved effortlessly among the Parisian avant-garde, becoming a friend of Guillaume Appollinaire, Pablo Picasso, Juan Gris, and Gertrude Stein. He claimed to have initiated the movement called Creationism even before Revérdy, and he engaged in many polemics about the matter throughout the years. Huidobro was, in fact, a polemicist in matters artistic and political, and once even ran (unsuccessfully) for the presidency of Chile.

Huidobro theorized about the kind of poetry he wrote, sometimes in the form of manifestos, affirming in his poem "Ars poetica" that the poet was a small god, who should create out of nothing realities to stand on an equal footing with other realities. He adds: "Why do you sing of the rose, oh poets! / Make it bloom in the poem." His "theory" is, in fact, the quite common avant-garde claim about the freedom of poetry to use language and poetic resources unconcerned for tradition or the demands of sense or meaning; the notion of the poet as a minor god goes back to the Romantics. In practice, however, Huidobro was quite original and wrote some of the major poems of Spanish-language Modernism.

One in particular, *Altazor* (1931), is the showpiece of Latin American Modernism and one of the greatest poems of the twentieth century. Huidobro claims to have written most of it in 1919. Fragments had appeared in journals before the first book-length edition, published in Madrid, which caused quite a splash and featured a portrait of the poet drawn by Picasso. The full title reads: *Altazor o el viaje en paracaídas. Poema en VII cantos (1919)* (Altazor or the Voyage in a Parachute: A Poem in VII Cantos (1919)). The title is a portmanteau word combining "alto," high, and "azor," goshawk, a bird of prey used in falconry;

"highhawk" might be a suitable translation. It suggests hunting at very high altitudes, which is the central conceit of the poem, whose subtending mythic story is that of Icarus; Huidobro's poem has this and much else, in common with Joyce's *Ulysses*, a work that is, at least in composition, its contemporary (the novel is from 1922). *Altazor* is an ambitious long poem; the first edition was 111 pages long.

The notion of this Icarus figure traveling in a parachute that is like an umbrella lends a humorous tone to the poem, an ironic distance. The idea of the fall, with all of its Christian resonances, also gives the poem an allegorical cast tempered by irony. The poem is like a series of dialogues the speaker holds with himself, with God, with the reader, or with an implicit interlocutor who seems to have asked questions. At times the poem becomes a long monologue about a variety of topics of the utmost seriousness, though their expression might seem humorous because of the many puns, repetitions, lists, anaphora, disconnected statements, and random words. There is a progression from canto to canto, though these are not of uniform length, and each varies, though not uniformly, in tone. The progress is toward the dissolution of language: the poem ends with a series of letters, presumably representing arbitrary sounds. Man is, according to the poem, "a metaphysical animal burdened with sorrows."

Thematically *Altazor* sometimes reads like Heidegger's *Being and Time* (1927) put to poetry, although it is difficult to conceive that Huidobro would have read the German philosopher. But the self represented in the poem has fallen into time and is in search of meaning in a world devoid of certainties of any kind. His existential quest, as he presumably soars, is for a way out of the anguish he feels; *angustia* (anguish) is a word used repeatedly in the poem. The speaker of Altazor is in a void, represented by infinite cosmic space and also the sea, but he is not in a historical vacuum. He rues that he has come into being when Christianity is dead and there is nothing to replace it. Europe has buried all of its dead, meaning World War I is over, and the repeated mention of new technologies, such as airplanes, gives the protagonist a context that is reminiscent of Futurism. These scientific discoveries, astronomy foremost among them, appear to announce possible answers and solutions, but they do not seem to be near.

Altazor is a complicated poem. It is not even consistently poetic. There are fragments that read like prose poems. Poetry, in fact, in the traditional sense, is the object of repeated mockery and is represented by musical instruments such as violins, violas, harps, and pianos, but never performing their given functions. Altazor, the speaker, acts as if possessed of a superior knowledge that allows him to know the secrets of things and the causes of events at a level that is beyond conventional poetic understanding. The world he describes is in a state of metamorphosis that is reminiscent of Ovid's. Things and beings are transformed by unusual reasons, and their resultant new appearance is expressed by words that are combinations of words, or words endowed with unconventional meanings. Altazor knows that he is trapped in language and tries mightily to work free of it by breaking it down and putting it back together with the glee a child would have doing the same to his toys. In one long sequence the word "mill" is paired with many different adjectives and prepositional phrases performing the turning and grinding of the device. The parallel with Joyce's *Ulysses* is clear, and so is the resemblance, thematically, to Eliot's *The Wasteland*.

Huidobro, for all his accomplishments and self-promotion, was soon upstaged by his compatriot Pablo Neruda (1904–73), a poetic volcano who became one of the leading poets of the twentieth century and a prominent political figure. Born in Temuco, a southern Chilean town, he changed his name, Ricardo Neftalí Reyes, to conceal from his father that he wrote poetry, taking Pablo as his first name in homage to Paul Valéry and borrowing the surname from the Czech novelist Jan Neruda. In 1921 he moved to Santiago to study French but devoted himself mostly to writing poetry and to the bohemian life. In 1923 he published his first book, *Crepusculario* (a combination of "crepuscular" and "calendar" evocative of Lugones's *Lunario sentimental*). *Veinte poemas de amor y una canción desesperada* (*Twenty Love Poems and a Song of Despair*) appeared the next year; it was to become a best seller throughout the Spanish-speaking world. No book of poetry has ever circulated more in Spanish. With his newly acquired fame, Neruda was able to secure a very minor diplomatic post as honorary consul in Burma. It was at least a chance to travel, and the beginning of a long career in the foreign service.

Neruda became a great and greatly acclaimed poet with a poem he wrote while in the East, *Residencia en la tierra* (*Residence on Earth*, 1933), which reflected his reading of English poetry (Blake) and the French symbolists and Surrealists as well as novelists like Proust and Joyce. Some believe that Neruda revolutionized Spanish verse as much as Darío had. The second, 1935 edition of *Residencia* (the first had been very small) was extremely influential in Latin America and Spain. These were poems with lines of varying lengths, mostly blank verse, and torrents of tropes that make them obscure, yet emotionally stirring. Some are starkly autobiographical and erotic, narrating the travails of a self alienated from the world and from itself, and desperately seeking communion with others and with nature: "I happen to tire of being a man."

The poems of *Residencia* were more powerful than anything the Surrealists or any other avant-garde poets ever wrote, perhaps because Neruda was closer to the romantic sources of the avant-garde. These poems represented a world in ruins, a "godless apocalypse" as Amado Alonso once put it. Their chaotic language seemed to express inchoate passions, fears, and desires in a language that seems appropriate to those moods, a language that is symphonic in its cadences and movement, as if the subconscious had found an idiom free from reason and conventional meanings. Named consul to Barcelona in 1934 and a year later to Madrid,

Neruda joined the poets of the Generation of 27, with whom he issued a journal, *Caballo verde para la poesía* (Green Horse for Poetry), and witnessed the beginning of the Spanish Civil War.

Neruda was dismissed as consul because of his political involvement, but he remained in Spain, where in 1937 he helped organize a congress of antifascist intellectuals and published *España en el corazón* (Spain in the Heart), his first book of political poems. This book would later be reprinted at the front lines in Barcelona on paper made by the soldiers from captured flags, rags, bloodied gauze, and other trophies of war. It is, with Vallejo's, the highpoint of political poetry in the language. In 1939, at the conclusion of the Civil War, a more sympathetic Chilean government sent Neruda to Paris as consul for Spanish emigration, with the mission of aiding refugees from the Spanish Republic by finding countries that would take them. After stints in Chile, Neruda wound up in Mexico, where he was named consul general.

When he left the Mexican capital to return again to Chile in 1943, he was given a farewell banquet attended by more than two thousand guests. In that year he published *Canto general de Chile* (General Song of Chile), which would become the *Canto general* (General Song) in 1950. On his way home he visited the pre-Incaic ruins of Macchu Picchu in Peru and in 1944 published *Alturas de Macchu Picchu* (The Heights of Macchu Picchu), which would also be incorporated into the *Canto general*. In 1944 he was elected senator and the next year joined the Chilean Communist Party; he would be an obedient member for the rest of his life. After a polemic with the Chilean president, Neruda escaped on horseback over the Andes to Argentina and later surfaced in Paris, bearing the passport of a friend, the Guatemalan novelist Miguel Ángel Asturias.

Neruda's *Canto general*, one of the highest poetic achievements of the twentieth century, was published in a special edition printed in Mexico City, with drawings by the great muralists Diego Rivera and David Alfaro Siqueiros. Neruda was then forty-six. The vast poem was a return to origins and a rebirth, a sweeping recollection that included not only memories of Neruda's intimate and poetic self but also the natural and collective history of Latin America. He gathers here his avant-garde experience, particularly the surrealist, and tempers it with the keen historical awareness forced on him by the political catastrophes of the 1930s and '40s. The poem expressed the hope that out of the ruins of Europe and of Western civilization in general, Latin America would emerge as a new, vital force, untainted by the errors and sins of the Old World. At the core of the *Canto general* is an effort to create an American myth, a version of American history that can constitute the cipher of American destiny. Because Neruda is a Romantic, that myth had to have as protagonist his own poetic self, the individual whose suffering and vision the myth will legitimize. Hence his journey through life is a story woven into the fabric of the poem, as is the evolution of the poetic voice within its fictive time.

"Canto general" means "general song," perhaps in contrast to Whitman's *Song of Myself*. A general song would be the song of all or about everything, meaning the objective, concrete world that we call real and the history of the world—the entire history of the world, reminiscent of the aspirations of general histories in colonial times. This is consistent with the sweep of the poem, which begins in pre-Hispanic America, or even prehistoric America, when humanity is just about to emerge from the clay, and moves along until it reaches the here and now of the poet writing in 1949. Perhaps a good translation of the title would be "Song of All," meaning the history and the concrete world but also the mind of man, his beliefs and ethics, his fears and aspirations. The poem is a solemn celebration of all, a chant in a major key. Its deep resonances come from its long, sonorous lines, occasionally broken by shorter ones for emphasis, and by its avalanche of metaphors. Neruda's poem is a cornucopia of tropes. Everything is in a state of flux, in the process of becoming something or of looking like something else. The analogue here is America's proliferating nature: "in fertility time grew." There is no conventional rhyme, meter, or strophic arrangement, and although the history recounted begins before the beginning of history, it does not flow chronologically from there until the end. The *Canto* establishes its own inner rhythms, like a liturgy being founded, its grandiose tropes not just naming but anointing things.

After the triumph of the *Canto general*, which also includes a paean to Stalin, Neruda began a series of extended trips through Europe as a sort of roving cultural ambassador representing the Communist Party. He also initiated a radical change in his poetry, toward a simpler mode of expression. In 1952 he published anonymously *Los versos del capitán* (The Captain's Verses), a collection of love poems, and in 1954 the first volume of his *Odas elementales* (*Elementary Odes*); three would appear in the 1950s. These were poems in which the poet wished to look anew at the humblest elements of reality, to isolate and celebrate with his gaze objects and beings normally left out of the purview of poetry—an onion, an artichoke, a cat.

In 1959, still in his role as itinerant poetic and political conscience of the Americas, Neruda traveled to Cuba and, as a result, wrote *Canción de gesta* (Epic Song), a poem in praise of the Revolution; later he would have a major quarrel with the cultural commissars of Castro's regime. But Neruda's next volumes of poetry, *Cantos ceremoniales* (Ceremonial Songs) and *Memorial de Isla Negra* (Isla Negra Memorial), turned inward and backward, to his childhood, to his life on the Chilean coast. In 1971 Neruda returned to Europe, now as Chilean ambassador to France, representing the government of his longtime friend Salvador Allende, who had been elected president. It was a year of hope and revolutionary plenitude, soon crowned by Neruda's long-expected Nobel Prize, which some believed had been delayed because of cold war politics. But now Neruda was ill with cancer. He returned to Chile in 1972 where he witnessed the downfall of Allende and died full of grief on September 23, 1973.

Another poet who went to Spain during the Civil War was also a Communist and wrote politically inspired poetry: the Cuban Nicolás Guillén (1902–89). A mulatto, Guillén was the leading figure of the Afro-Cuban movement, which began in the mid-twenties as an exaltation of the African component of Cuban culture. It involved composers, poets, and novelists and was chiefly a poetic movement. Guillén incorporated into his verse rhythms that mimicked those of popular Afro-Cuban music and words derived from the African languages spoken on the island: these languages were mostly liturgical, for ritualistic use. In Spanish they sounded odd, like meaningless combinations of sound similar to those used by Huidobro. They did have a meaning, however, even if the reader did not understand it, and they provided a beat. Guillén's first and most famous book was *Motivos de son* (Song Motifs, 1930), which caused quite a stir in Cuba and the rest of the Antilles. The title is clever. "Motivo" means "motif," as in musical motif, but it also means motive or reason for something. Thus the title could be taken to mean "reasons for this kind of *son*." "Son" is a kind of popular Cuban music, but it also means "music" in general, and is the third-person plural of the verb "to be." The poems in the book are equally sophisticated, though at first they do not seem to be. They are very theatrical, dramatizing dialogues, sometimes comical, among characters, often a man and a woman.

Guillén adapted Modernist techniques to create poetry that sounds Afro-Cuban. His success was great because he was a very good poet, not just because of the Afro-Cuban inflection of his poetry. In books like *Sóngoro cosongo* (1931), *West Indies Ltd.* (1934), and *Cantos para soldados y sones para turistas* (Songs for Soldiers and *sones* for Tourists, 1937), Guillén's poetry became increasingly political. In Spain, where his poetry acquired a more international dimension, he published *España: poema en cuatro angustias y una esperanza* (Spain: a Poem in Four Anguishes and One Hope, 1937). In 1937 he attended the antifascist congress in Valencia organized by Neruda. Guillén, a Communist since the

1930s, joined the Castro regime when it came to power and served as president of the Writers' Union until his death.

A very young Octavio Paz (Mexico, 1914–98) was also at that congress in Valencia with Neruda, Guillén, and many others. He was destined to become the next Latin American poet to win the Nobel Prize and Neruda's antagonist, both in poetry and in politics. Paz went to Spain as a politically committed intellectual with Marxist leanings and left-wing connections. One of his first books, *¡No pasarán!* (They Shall not Pass!, 1936) takes as its title one of the slogans of the Republican cause in Spain. Back in Mexico he broke with the Left as a result of the Nazi-Soviet Pact of 1939, and became a bitter and persistent critic of Communism for the rest of his life. He founded two important journals in the 1940s, *Taller* and *El hijo pródigo*, and in 1943, thanks to a Guggenheim Fellowship, he moved to the United States for two years, living first in California and later in New York. In 1945 Paz began his diplomatic career with a post in Paris, where he was associated with André Breton and what was left of the Surrealist movement in France.

He returned to Mexico at the end of the decade and was involved with the Spanish writers and intellectuals who had settled there having fled the Franco regime. This group was made up of disciples of José Ortega y Gasset, the Spanish philosopher who had become a follower of Heidegger after the 1920s. The Spaniards in Mexico were Heideggerians, with one, José Gaos, publishing a translation of *Being and Time* in 1949. While Paz would be influenced by other tendencies, mainly Eastern philosophies as a result of his trip to Japan and India in the early fifties, Surrealism and Existentialism were the main influences in his intellectual development. Paz found in Eastern religions a way to translate existentialism into a language with liturgical substance, but without the ideological ballast of the West, which seemed to have been emptied by Heidegger (and earlier by Nietzsche). The void of being can be filled with poetry, a poetry whose configuration is given by a set of beliefs that is alien, yet compelling, a poetic religion that can be the mirror of being. The pull of the East had been felt since Romanticism, but Paz managed to assimilate it without turning it into something exotic.

With the publication of his essay *El laberinto de la soledad* (*The Labyrinth of Solitude*, 1950), a brilliant interpretation of the Mexican character, Paz had become by the 1950s a very visible public intellectual. In that decade he also published his most ambitious attempt at a poetic theory in *El arco y la lira* (*The Bow and the Lyre*, 1956), the most sophisticated statement in Spanish on the topic. This was followed by *Los hijos del limo* (*Children of the Mire*, 1974), a major proposal about the origin and evolution of modern Latin American poetry. His poetic production did not lag behind. In fact, it was during this period that Paz published his most significant volumes of poetry, *Libertad bajo palabra* (Freedom under Parole, 1949), and *Piedra de sol* (*Sunstone*); the latter incorporated the Aztec calendar into a profound meditation on the meaning of time and history. These were followed by many books that make up a substantial poetic oeuvre. The central poem, however, is *Sunstone* because it is a synthesis of Paz's major topics, from the precariousness of the self, caught in the void of existence in time, to eroticism, derived in part from the Far East, to the nature of poetry. With *Altazor* and *Canto general*, *Sunstone* is one of the three peaks of modern Latin American poetry, and among the major poems of the twentieth century.

In *Sunstone* a nameless voice appears to be falling through space and time. Falling is a major trope in the poem, reminiscent of *Altazor* and related to Heidegger's notion of the self as being in a fallen state. But falling is also part of the cosmic resonances of the poem, a Dantesque tumbling through the heavens. Dante is also present in the erotic desire animating the journey and sustaining the self through it. The anxious poetic voice seeks connectedness, communion, as the cosmic debris of historical catastrophes floats by: we were by then in the space age. Love looms as the only salvation; but desire must become incarnate in the here and now, a present in which physical love will provide a momentary sense of order, a flash of plenitude. Two bodies, naked and intertwined, leap over the gap of time, they are invulnerable, nothing can touch them, they return to the source in each other, through each other, there is no longer you, nor I, no tomorrow, no yesterday, no names, the truth of two in a single body, a single soul, total being achieved in the instant of love.

But violence and sacrifice appear as offerings to hungry and demanding gods. Christian and Aztec mythology furnish the context here. Mythology is given historical embodiment in the figures of Lincoln, Moctezuma, Trotsky, and the slain president of Mexico, Francisco Madero, all leaders assassinated in the pursuit of good. Eros and good are held in precarious balance. At the end of the poem the opening lines are repeated. Unable to reach the lasting plenitude it seeks, the voice falls into repetition, a physical, sexual repetition that joins together disparate echoes in the reader's mind and provides a momentary bliss; a recognition of sorts. The repetition also signals the cosmological structure of *Sunstone*. The poem's 584 lines reflect the Aztec calendar's period, as well as the synodical period of the planet Venus (the time between two successive conjunctions of the planet with the sun). Goddess of love in Western mythology, Venus is the guiding star; the voice's fall through time was always measured by eros.

Sunstone contains the master plot of Paz's poetry and of his vision of history. Denuded of its verbal finery, the plot appears reductive. But it is far from it in the poetic texts themselves, in the drama of poetic self-creation. Paz was a poet who lived in and through desire, through nostalgia for sacredness, a sacredness that is briefly revealed in the ruins of ancient religions or in quivering bodies by ever-present love. That master plot continues to furnish the subtext of poems written in the 1960s and '70s in which there is an increasing appearance of the city as the site of historical catastrophe and of the East as a landscape strewn with ruins left by colonialism but also as a place in which a sense of the sacred abides. Utopia remains an erotic feast. The copulating figures in Indian architecture defy the shattering effect of history and return to an origin in which the poet can reinvest the ruins with sacredness.

In his 1960 book, *Homenaje y profanación* (*Homage and desecrations*) Paz rewrote "Constant Love beyond Death," a sonnet by Quevedo, thereby claiming as his poetic precursors the baroque poets of the seventeenth century, whose echoes were audible in his poetry much earlier. His return to the baroque is emblematic. Realizing that the language inherited from the Spanish-language Romantics was derivative and hollow, modern Spanish poets reached back to Quevedo, and above all to his contemporary and bitter enemy Luis de Góngora and their disciples as the only worthy models, poets who had achieved an original poetic revolution. Paz is torn between the glittering imagistic world of Góngora, who became the patron saint of the Generation of 27 poets, and the wit, paradox, and sober vision of Quevedo, but he seems to settle finally on the latter as a mentor, as well as on the seventeenth-century Mexican nun and poet Sor Juana Inés de la Cruz, whose biography he wrote. Quevedo's language, oscillating between excrement and the most purified love, repulsion and desire, is particularly appropriate for Paz's sense of the failure of history.

Paz served as ambassador to India until 1968 when he resigned in protest against the government's massacre of students at the Tlatelolco Plaza in Mexico City. He returned to Mexico, where he remained an influential literary and political figure through his new journal, *Vuelta*, a splendid artistic magazine that became the leading such publication in the Spanish-speaking world. He also traveled abroad, again in the role as international literary celebrity that he had inherited from Darío and shared with Neruda until the latter's death. When the superb group of Latin American novelists who brought about what is known as the "Boom" of the Latin

American novel emerged, Paz joined them as part of a very visible jet set of literary luminaries. He quarreled with some of them for their support of the Castro regime in Cuba and other left-wing causes, and he celebrated the collapse of the Soviet Union in 1990. It was probably Paz's courageous denunciations of Communism and its fellow travelers that delayed his reception of the Nobel Prize, which finally occurred in 1990, when he was seventy-six.

The Cuban José Lezama Lima (1910–76), who was probably as great a poet if not greater than Paz, lived in relative obscurity in his native Havana, a city he deeply loved and rarely left, even for other cities on the island. He is the perfect example of a writer who, because he was so steeped in his own language and so innovative in his work, was recognized only by a small group of admirers for most of his life. In Cuba, Lezama did have around him a coterie of friends and associates whom he led. It came to be known as the *Orígenes* group after the magazine by that name that Lezama published with his fellow poet José Rodríguez Feo. *Orígenes* ran from 1944 to 1954, publishing major writers from Latin America and translations of such important figures from abroad as Wallace Stevens. It was a wonderful journal, uncompromising in its devotion to art and with a generally Roman Catholic orientation. Among Lezama's eccentricities, from the perspective of Modernism, was his Catholicism. But the most relevant was his extremely obscure manner of expression, be it in conversation or in his writings, be they in prose or poetry, obstinate as they are in their pursuit of truth and beauty at the expense of intelligibility. But once Lezama's idiom is accepted, the splendor of his work shines through: it is perhaps the most original in the Spanish language since the time of Cervantes and Góngora.

Lezama wrote in that idiom from the very first poem, *Muerte de Narciso* (Death of Narcissus), to the last, *Fragmentos a su imán* (Magnet's Shards, 1977), as well as in his most famous book, the novel *Paradiso* (Paradiso, 1966). In contrast to most Latin American writers of note, Lezama was neither a cosmopolitan nor a polyglot. He traveled only briefly to Jamaica and Mexico, was never in Paris, and Spanish was his only language, though he could presumably make his way reading French. All of his readings, which were vast and idiosyncratic, were in Spanish, but his erudition was stupendous, if capricious. He was knowledgeable in the fathers of the church and knew the Spanish classics, major and minor, in excruciating detail. He was steeped in Latin American literature from the colonial period to his day, being in touch through *Orígenes* with the writing, particularly poetry, being done in other countries. Contemporary Spanish poets he knew intimately, sometimes personally as they came to Havana as a result of the Civil War. Juan Ramón Jiménez, who spent some months in the Cuban capital in 1937, grew fond of the young Lezama. Cuban poets flocked around Lezama, hoping to be published in his journal. Lezama lived in relative obscurity before the Revolution and was harassed by the commissars after the Communist government took over.

Lezama rejected the major ideological trends of Modernism: he was not a Marxist, rejected Freudianism (for him psychoanalysis turned a stage of human development into a system); disdained existentialism (man is not for death, as Heidegger proclaimed, but for resurrection), and was oblivious to the "isms" of the avant-garde. His language is prelapsarian, meaning that it is a language written before the Fall, before original sin, before the law. Hence Lezama is careless with his spelling, cavalier with his citations, and his syntax is sinuous, like Proust's, but not deliberately elegant. Lezama mixes rhetorical registers, blending the high with the low, the vulgar with the sublime. Shedding the prejudices inherent in all the ideologies and trends mentioned is difficult for the reader, but in doing so Lezama's universe appears coherent and systematic. The key notion is the "hypertelic," or that which takes place beyond the end, beyond intention, beyond structure, limits, or goals. That is the realm of poetry or of art in general, and obviously also the realm of resurrection, that which emerges after death, the most definitive of boundaries. It is a poetics of superfluity and excess, which is the reason why Lezama so admired the baroque and made its tenets his own.

A survivor of the avant-garde and a major poet, who was overshadowed by giants like Neruda, Vallejo, and Paz, is Nicanor Parra, born in 1914 in Santiago, Chile. Parra followed a different route to poetry. He was originally a theoretical physicist, a subject he studied at Brown University in Rhode Island, among other institutions, and taught at the university level in Chile and elsewhere. The chief trait Parra picked up from the avant-garde was a playful humor that makes him unique in Latin American poetry, and that anticipates the novels of the Boom, where it first appears consistently in fiction. Charlie Chaplin was among Parra's masters, and like Chaplin Parra projected the image of an eager, fumbling individual trying to assert himself with feeble powers and abilities, who stumbles upon the obstacles reality places in his way. One of his most important poems is "Soliloquio del individuo" (Soliloquy of the Individual). It is a long poem that mocks the very idea of the individual self by telling in a sardonic tone what amounts to the entire history of the human race as told by this funny fellow who lists, deadpan, the major moments in human development as if he had lived through them all. The recurring refrain is "I am the individual," which is a hollow boast given that things seem to happen to him, to not be his doing. It is an anti-Whitmanian poem and hence an anti-Nerudian poem. In contrast to his distinguished fellow Chilean, Parra abhorred rhetoric and poked fun at the poetic tics and tricks of Modernism, favoring instead popular musical and poetic forms, such as the *cueca*, a Chilean kind of song and dance. *Poemas y antipoemas* (*Poems and Antipoems*, 1954) is Parra's best-known collection.

Parra was accompanied in today's Chile by yet another survivor of the avant-garde, a major poet in his own right, Gonzalo Rojas, born in 1917 and the recipient of many literary prizes, who died on April 25, 2011. Rojas was a presence in Chile and the rest of Latin America, known for his having founded the Surrealist group in the 1930s and for his years of exile during Pinochet's dictatorship, when he roamed the world (Germany, the United States, Mexico) as the new ambassador for Latin American poetry. Equidistant from Neruda and Parra, Rojas sounds at times very Baudelairian in his complaints about the ravages of time (one of his collections is called *Contra la muerte* (Against Death, 1964), but yet more optimistic and whimsical, as in his poem "Al silencio" (To Silence), in which silence is portrayed as the all-encompassing voice of the cosmos.

When Paz died in 1998, the chapter was closed on Latin American poetry of the twentieth century. No poet of his stature was left at that time, and none has emerged since. It was a remarkable century of poetry that began with the disciples of Rubén Darío and ended with poets like Lezama and Paz, who had overcome the master of Modernismo, but were still true to Darío's devotion to the pursuit of beauty and the rigorous cultivation of poetic language. Darío is still revered in Latin America, even if his fame has not transcended the Spanish language.

Chapter 5
Latin American fiction in the twentieth century: Regionalism to Modernism

Prose fiction, except for the short story, fell behind poetry in the evolution of Latin American arts toward Modernism in the early part of the twentieth century; there were no equivalents to Pablo Neruda, César Vallejo, or Gabriela Mistral until the 1940s. In spite of the existence of a group of distinguished regionalist novelists, modern Latin American literature was thought to be then preeminently a literature of poets. Neruda and Mistral, with international recognition and living in countries like Spain, France, and the United States, drew most of the public attention.

When the novelists who brought about what has come to be known as the Boom of the Latin American novel changed this radically in the 1960s, it was because prose fiction caught up with the poetry, incorporating Modernist narrative techniques. It was not a sudden development, as the word would suggest, but a gradual one that began, tentatively in the thirties and forties, accelerated in the fifties, and came to full bloom in the sixties. Latin American fiction then contributed original features to the modern novel in the West, but this was partly due to its belated adoption of practices that had been common since Proust, Kafka, Joyce, and Faulkner. By the twenty-first century, Latin American prose fiction was in step with the rest of literature in the West, a full participant in the international, indeed global commerce of the arts.

In the early twentieth century, the Latin American short story continued under the sway of Rubén Darío and Modernismo. The new short-story writers were still intensely concerned with form, and their successors have continued to be so because, like poetry, the short story relies on the deployment of exacting techniques under the pressure of the need for brevity. Some of the short-story writers, like Leopoldo Lugones, were also poets. The most accomplished and influential writer of the period was the Uruguayan Horacio Quiroga (1878–1937), who wrote, perhaps tongue in cheek, a much-quoted "Decalogue of the Perfect Short Story Writer" (1917). The ambience of perversion, the ghoulishness, the presence of disease of both mind and body permeate Quiroga's fiction and reveal the pervasive influence of Edgar Allan Poe.

Quiroga's own life was fraught with violence: his father died in a hunting accident, and his stepfather committed suicide, as did Quiroga's wife, and ultimately he himself, when he was terminally ill with cancer. Quiroga spent the requisite season in Paris but returned to live in the tropical jungle of Misiones in northern Argentina. Devoid of sentimentality and local color, his stories, are stark, tragic, shocking in their themes and rigorous execution. *Cuentos de amor de locura y de muerte* (Stories about Love, Madness, and Death) appeared in 1917, and *Cuentos de la selva* (Jungle Stories, translated as *South American Jungle Tales*) in 1918. In Quiroga's stories the exquisite Modernista aesthetic has been cast aside to face the violent, turbulent natural and human landscape of Latin America with astonishing results. He continues to be regarded as a master of the genre, admired and imitated by writers of subsequent generations.

The natural and human landscape of Latin America was the setting for the vast, ambitious novels that dominated the first half of the twentieth century. Quiroga may have had an impact on some of their authors, but the aesthetics of these books were quite different from his. These were books that largely adhered to the tenets of nineteenth-century realism and were oblivious to the changes brought about by Modernism in the novel. They were concerned with the uniqueness of individual countries owing to their peculiar natural features, mainly their geography, and how the available resources were exploited. It was implicit that the "earth," that nature, determined the character of each nation, that it was a cipher of its social and political destiny. Hence they are known as *novelas de la tierra*, or "novels about or of the earth." Their authors had at heart an anthropological mission: to probe the culture of their nation by studying its folklore, its linguistic peculiarities, its beliefs, myths, and even popular poetry, and to provide a synthesis, an interpretation of that culture. Also, these authors, who were typically from the capital, went to the countryside to explore the ways of the folk, as their precursors the *costumbristas* had done in the nineteenth century, but now armed with more refined techniques derived from the developing social sciences.

The novels were the fictional counterpart of an entire movement in modern Latin American literature to find the cultural identity of individual countries and, also, of the whole of Latin America. This tendency developed in the wake of Sarmiento and especially Rodó and his "Ariel," which was a great success. Soon there followed essays by such academics as the distinguished Dominican essayist Pedro Henríquez Ureña, the Marxist Peruvian José Carlos Mariátegui, the Mexican intellectual and statesman Samuel Ramos, and many others. The trend culminated with *El laberinto de la soledad* (*The Labyrinth of Solitude*, 1950), by the Mexican poet Octavio Paz, and "La expresión americana" (American Expression, 1957), by the Cuban poet José Lezama Lima. Paz's psychoanalytic approach, in which he cast Spanish conqueror Hernán Cortés as the violent father of Mexico, and his Indian mistress and interpreter La Malinche as the ravaged mother, was enormously popular and influential.

The prevalence of the topic of national identity in the essay and other genres has abated somewhat, but in the first half of the twentieth century it was the dominant one in Latin American literature, particularly in the novel, where the analyses were protracted and presumably based on firsthand observation, like that of an ethnographer (in reality, the writers rarely ventured too far from their homes).

Study of the countryside would presumably yield a kind of knowledge that could lead to a cleansing of the deviations that had accrued in the corrupted cities, a variation of the pastoral outlook hearkening back to classical times. The popularity of the novelas de la tierra was great and enduring, and their production through all the Latin American countries extensive. The trend was led by three writers, Ricardo Güiraldes (Argentina, 1886–1927), José Eustasio Rivera (Colombia, 1888–1928), and Rómulo Gallegos (Venezuela, 1884–1969).

Güiraldes, who spent his early years in Paris and is reputed to have learned French before Spanish, was a link to the avant-garde, having founded two magazines, *Martín Fierro* and *Proa*, that promoted the new movements. His reputation, however, was established by the novel *Don Segundo Sombra* (1926), with which he created an Argentine literary myth, that of the old gaucho. The novel is a paean to the booming cattle industry in Argentina (the source of Güiraldes' family's considerable wealth), with Don Segundo, the old gaucho, as a key figure. He embodies the wisdom of the countryside, acquired in the demanding work of the cowboy, and passes it on to a young man from the city.

The story is a *bildungsroman*, a novel of education, and an elegy. *Don Segundo Sombra* is a reprise of José Hernández's gaucho epic *Martín Fierro* and a deliberate intervention into the debate about the Argentine character that the poem had sparked. It concludes with Don Segundo going away on his horse, over a hill, and the narrator, the young man who is now a ranch owner like his father, writing that seeing him leave felt like a bleeding. Don Segundo had advised his apprentice gaucho "Be tough, boy." The labors of the pampas harden the Argentine soul. *Don Segundo Sombra* transcended Argentina, however, both because other Latin Americans could identify with the kind of folk wisdom and stoicism of the protagonist and because of the novel's many aesthetic virtues, not the least of which is its lyricism.

Rivera was a bohemian poet who fell prey to the decadent elements of Modernismo and lived a short, intense life hounded by health problems and obsessed by the lack of recognition for his novel, *La vorágine* (*The Vortex*, 1924). A lawyer, he was named to the commission assessing boundary disputes between Venezuela and Colombia, and he traveled to the jungle to study the situation. There he was appalled by the conditions endured by the workers of the rubber plantations. This experience, and probably readings of European explorers and perhaps even of Conrad's *Heart of Darkness*, led him to write *La vorágine*. In it, Arturo Cova, the protagonist, escapes to the jungle with his lover only to find a world of violence and disease. It is in a hallucinatory state that he writes what purportedly will become the text of the novel. The plot leads him progressively farther into a kind of tropical hell from which he cannot escape, and eventually, as the ending of the novel reads, "The jungle swallowed them."

Rivera's Romantic imagination allows him to make sublime descriptions of the brutal natural world and of the pitiless relations among the characters, including a particularly compelling woman who seduces Cova with her wiles and frenzied sexuality. He feels himself slide down a path of degradation and mental instability in which all values vanish. *La vorágine* is a ruthless book without the idealizations of *Don Segundo Sombra*, a novel of social and political protest that, beyond the novela de la tierra, founded another subgenre, that of the *novela de la selva,* or "novel of the jungle."

Of all the novelas de la tierra the prototypical one is Gallegos's *Doña Bárbara* (1929). It is the one that most directly engages the Latin American literary tradition and that had the greatest impact on subsequent Latin American writing. In the protagonist, Doña Bárbara, Gallegos created another literary myth, with greater reach than Güiraldes's Don Segundo Sombra. Gallegos himself gained international acclaim when he published the novel, becoming the first Latin American novelist to do so. A liberal with a commitment to popular education (he had been a teacher), Gallegos opposed the Venezuelan dictator Juan Vicente Gómez (in power from 1909 to 1935) and suffered exile in New York and Mexico, among other places. In 1948, during a period of democratic rule, he was elected president of Venezuela but was deposed within the year by a military coup, which eventually brought to power Marcos Pérez Jiménez, who governed with an iron hand until 1958. Gallegos spent those years in Cuba, the United States, and Mexico, countries in which he was much admired. In Mexico, *Doña Bárbara* was turned into a film with the Mexican star actress María Félix in the leading role.

Doña Bárbara is a long novel that dramatizes the conflict between civilization and barbarism at the core of Latin American culture proposed by Sarmiento in his *Facundo*. The very fact that the protagonist is called Doña Bárbara indicates that the story is allegorical; her lover's name is Santos Luzardo ("luz" means light). She rules a vast tract of the Venezuelan plain, the *llano*, which she has progressively acquired by illicit means, and using her potent sex appeal (she is known as "la devoradora de hombres," the devourer of men). Luzardo, legal heir to the land, has come back to it from Caracas, where he has become a lawyer. Their struggle, which turns into love, makes up the plot of the novel. Santos wants to bring the law and barbed wire to the llanos, and intends to stop the practice of fraudulent branding of cattle to restore order and regain his property. He is put to the test by Doña Bárbara´s men, who consider him a softie from the city, but he proves them wrong by showing off his skill as a horseman. Santos eventually prevails.

But the allure of the "barbarous," embodied by Doña Bárbara, is such that it becomes more attractive than the liberal ideology propounded by Gallegos through his male protagonist. In any case, in spite of the conventional cast of the novel, the conflicts dramatized by the protagonists take on a mythic aura that involves the very writing of the novel, which appears to be related to the branding of cattle and the parceling of the land with barbed wire. The law, as represented by these activities, seems to be subverted by their very violence. This makes *Doña Bárbara* a very compelling text that would be rediscovered by younger writers after it had been dismissed by those immediately following. Gallegos was most probably unaware of these repercussions in his novel, though he did write others with equally powerful forces at play.

A concomitant development to the novela de la tierra was the novel of the Mexican Revolution. The revolution had wide repercussions all over Latin America, and the mural art that developed as a result of it was very influential in the region. But so were novels about the revolution that began to be written during its unfolding and continued to appear in the 1940s, '50s, and even '60s. These novels also followed the patterns of nineteenth-century realism, but necessarily had an epic component. Martín Luis Guzmán (1887–1986), for instance, wrote prolix chronicle-like novels like *El águila y la serpiente* (The Eagle and the Serpent, 1928) and *La sombra del caudillo* (The Caudillo's Shadow, 1929) about the revolution and the political turmoil that followed. The best of the novelists of the Mexican Revolution, however, was Mariano Azuela (1873–1952), whose *Los de abajo* (*The Underdogs*, 1915) became a classic of Latin American literature.

A physician, Azuela joined the forces of Julián Medina, a Pancho Villa follower, serving as field doctor. Later he was exiled to El Paso, Texas, where he wrote *Los de abajo*. The protagonist is Demetrio Macías, a peasant, who joins a group fighting against the Federales of Victoriano Huerta. The Federales take or destroy their property, steal their wives, and kill indiscriminately. Macías's men are no better. When they take a town they loot and kill, oblivious to any ideals. In the end Macías recognizes that he is acting without aim and compares himself, in a memorable scene, to a stone he throws down a canyon and sees bounce here and there toward the bottom. Azuela is a skillful narrator whose chief virtue is the starkness of his descriptions and his concentration on the action. After his return to Mexico he was recognized as a great writer and awarded literary prizes. No Mexican writer has bested Azuela as a narrator, and *Los de abajo,* together with Juan Rulfo's *Pedro Páramo,* are the best Mexican novels of all time and among the best from Latin America.

The Latin American novel, however, was straitjacketed by the constraints of nineteenth-century realism: a third-person, omniscient narrator who views reality from the perspective of bourgeois common sense, a prose that tries not to be dissonant or call attention to itself; a plot that follows consecutively without interruptions toward an end that is consistent with the preceding action. The way out of this discursive prison was to allow the voices of the strange folk depicted to resonate, to invade the text with their quirks, discord, and noise. This is precisely what two novelists from different Latin American countries who met in Paris would do: the Guatemalan Miguel Ángel Asturias (1899–1974) and the Cuban Alejo Carpentier (1904–80). Asturias won the Nobel Prize in 1967, the first Latin American novelist to do so.

Carpentier, of Franco-Russian origin, had been born in Lausanne, Switzerland, but claimed throughout his life to have been born in Havana, where his parents had settled sometime after his birth and where he grew up. He was one of the founders of the Afro-Cuban movement that sought to exalt the African component of Cuban culture by incorporating some of its features into the arts, mostly poetry and music. Carpentier, who had training in music and was attuned to the Parisian avant-garde, wrote about painting, music, and literature. He also produced librettos for Afro-Cuban ballets and scripts for musical theater. He participated in political opposition to President Gerardo Machado, who had extended his presidential term by changing the constitution and who persecuted those who opposed him, particularly university students. Carpentier left for Paris in 1928, where he joined the Surrealist group led by André Breton and was involved in some of their squabbles. He continued writing musical theater, even some poetry, all in the Afro-Cuban vein, as well as one short story, which he wrote and published in French.

Carpentier was also writing an Afro-Cuban novel in which he attempted to incorporate some of the innovations of Cubism, Futurism, and Surrealism. The action was set in a sugar-mill town and in the marginal neighborhoods of Havana, populated by blacks. It was going to be, then, a regionalist novel—a novela de la tierra—focused on the countryside and the main industry of Cuba. The plot follows the life of Menegildo Cué, a young black who kills another for a woman, winds up in a Havana jail, and is killed in a brawl between two warring Afro-Cuban gangs. The action is interrupted by descriptive scenes written in staccato rhythm, without prepositions or transitions, replicating the beat of the machines of the mill or the music of a ritual. The black characters speak in their peculiar dialects, reproduced phonetically. There is a lavish dramatization of an initiation ceremony into one of the gangs, which belong to competing religious sects, and even pictures of the ceremonial objects and foods. Called *¡Écue-Yamba-O!* (Lord, Praised be Thou, in one of the African languages), the book has many of the makings of an ethnographic treatise. The novel, published in Madrid by a small house, did not have much impact and later, when he had become one of the greatest novelists in the world, Carpentier dismissed it as a failed experiment. It may have been, but it had pointed the way out of the aesthetics of realist fiction.

Asturias had better luck, perhaps because he waited nearly twenty years to publish his novel, *El señor presidente* (1946). He was of Mayan and Spanish ancestry, and in his childhood Estrada

Cabrera's harsh dictatorship had forced his family to move from Guatemala City to the countryside, where he came into contact with Indian cultures. But it was not until he studied Mayan culture at the Sorbonne that Asturias really learned about it. He translated the sacred book of the Mayas, the *Popol Vuh*, into Spanish but from a French translation, and in 1930 published *Leyendas de Guatemala* (Legends of Guatemala), a compilation of brief mythic stories. It was a great success and had the honor of a prologue by Paul Valéry. This book made Asturias's reputation, and it continued to suggest that Latin American fiction should assimilate the cultures of the region's non-European populations. It is still considered, with good reason, a superb book, and one of the turning points in the history of the Latin American short story, like Quiroga's collections. Alongside Carpentier, Asturias had also been writing his own novel, based on Estrada Cabrera's dictatorship and integrating into its composition some of the procedures of avant-garde poetry and art, particularly of Surrealism. *El señor presidente* became at once a classic of Latin American literature and the creator (or continuator, if one takes *Facundo* into account) of yet another literary myth, the dictator, and of a new subgenre, the dictator novel.

El señor presidente takes place in an unnamed country, and while the action is based on the activities of Estrada Cabrera and his henchmen, there are no real names in the novel. It is history on the verge of becoming myth, with characters that possess exaggerated features that make them grotesque to the point of unreality. There is an air of masquerade in the novel; some scenes are like something out of a nightmare. These effects are produced by the language, which is sometimes comprised of obsessive repetitions and of words that are created from the echoes of others, as well as onomatopoeias, like the very first sentence of the novel: "!Alumbra, lumbre de alumbre, Luzbel de piedralumbre! (Shine, shining light of alum, Lucifer of shining stone!). These are Surrealist tricks, reminiscent of automatic writing, or of the untamed language of the subconscious. The dictator is larger than life in his evilness, almost a figure out of a baroque *auto sacramental*, the allegorical one-act plays in which various kinds of sins are represented. There is a great deal of Roman Catholic lore in the novel, often parodied. Cara de Ángel, "Angel Face," is a diabolical, shifty character that combines beauty and perversion, and plays off the sexual desires of others. *El señor presidente* is not a doctrinaire novel, as there is no apparent source of all the wickedness, which at times seems to be gratuitous and endemic to the human condition. Sadism has almost an aesthetic appeal, to be part of a decadent society that consumes itself by its penchant for evil. The mythic element increased in Asturias's next novel, perhaps his masterpiece, *Hombres de maíz* (*Men of Maize*), drawn from Mayan lore, and with characters that altogether abandon realist conventions, something that did not quite happen in *El señor presidente*.

Asturias's innovations were nearly contemporary with those of five writers who are considered forerunners of the Boom of the Latin American novel in the 1960s, and who should rightly be considered as part of it: Jorge Luis Borges (Argentina, 1899–1986), Carpentier, Juan Carlos Onetti (Uruguay, 1909–94), Augusto Roa Bastos (Paraguay, 1917–2005), and Juan Rulfo (Mexico, 1918–86). It must be stated, in fact, that all of these writers were not only of as high a quality as their disciples, but better. This is particularly so in the cases of Borges, Carpentier, and Rulfo. Onetti and Roa Bastos had discovered Modernist writing and adopted some of its techniques. Onetti, who in 1980 received the Miguel de Cervantes Prize in Spain, the most prestigious in the Spanish language, was an early Latin American disciple of William Faulkner. His best-known novel is *El astillero* (*The Shipyard*, 1961), but *La vida breve* (*A Brief Life*, 1959) is also well known and highly regarded. He uses several unreliable narrators who tell the same story in different ways, and creates in the town of Santa María a self-sufficient fictional world. There is a sense of doom and an air of degradation in Onetti's world that is reminiscent of Dostoyevsky and even Louis Ferdinand Céline.

Roa Bastos is even more experimental, particularly in his masterpiece *Yo el Supremo* (*I the Supreme*, 1974). He too won the Miguel de Cervantes Prize, in 1990. Persecuted by the tyrant Alfredo Stroessner, Roa Bastos spent many years in exile, first in Buenos Aires and later in Paris. He was keenly concerned with the plight of the Guaraní Indians in Paraguay, many of whom are not Spanish speakers, and hence he was obsessed with the topic of the Spanish conquest. But in *Yo el Supremo* he follows Asturias's dictator-novel plan and Sarmiento's *Facundo* to focus on the rule of José Gaspar Rodríguez de Francia in Paraguay (1814–40). It is also an exploration of Stroessner's rule. But the novel is at the same time a very elaborate exploration of the relationship of writing to power, following the most advanced literary theories of the 1960s and 1970s. Neither Onetti nor Roa Bastos had anything to envy in the Boom novelists with whom they shared the limelight.

A reclusive, self-effacing, and self-destructive man, Rulfo was fanatical about artistic perfection and integrity. He published only two slim books, but they are both masterpieces. One, a short-story collection, *El llano en llamas* (*The Burning Plain*, 1953), is a highpoint in the history of the Latin American short story, along with books by Quiroga, Asturias, Borges, and Carpentier. His novel *Pedro Páramo* (1955) is considered by many the best Latin American novel. It is set in provincial Mexico in the aftermath of the revolution (1910–17). The fictional town Comala (a *comal* is the pan-like utensil to make tortillas) is ruled by Pedro Páramo, a caudillo who controls the lives of all the inhabitants and is consumed by his love for Susana San Juan. His son Juan Preciado has come back looking for his father and finds a village in which he learns in fragmented narratives, sometimes in the monologues of characters who are already dead, the tragic history of the region and his origins. *Pedro Páramo* is an intricately wrought novel in which the imprint of Faulkner is clear, but some have seen it as reminiscent of Dante's *Inferno*. Like the postbellum South described by the American master, Comala is a rural community living after an upheaval that unleashed the violence inherent in the human condition. Comala is a doomed world, and the tone of Rulfo's prose is one of resignation.

The starkness in Rulfo's narrative is consonant with that of the ambience of his fictional town and the attitudes of his characters. Comala is a rocky realm, and at the end, when Páramo dies, he crumbles to the ground like a pile of stones. There are mythic overtones in Juan Preciado's search for his father, in Pedro Páramo's patriarchal rule, which seems biblical, and in the relationship between the earth and the people. No translation has been able to capture Rulfo's language, so imbedded in Mexican speech patterns, so archaic and rooted in the essence of Spanish. Only Proust, Joyce, and Faulkner have managed to similarly plumb the depths of their own languages to produce their inimitable prose and to create their unique fictional universes.

Carpentier waited until 1949, sixteen years after *!Écue-Yamba-O!*, to publish another novel, *El reino de este mundo* (*The Kingdom of This World*). In that period he reinvented himself as a writer and came up with a formula that was not only a success for him but that also had a lasting impact on Latin American fiction. Carpentier found that the history of Latin America was the apposite subject for Latin American fiction, and that that history was contained in the chronicles of the discovery and conquest of the New World as well as in the myriad historical documents, the treasure trove of papers contained in libraries and archives. That history was full of characters, many of them minor actors, whose deeds were of the utmost interest for writers of fiction. Carpentier made this discovery as he conducted research to write a history of Cuban music, which he published in 1946. He also found that those documents were written in an archaic language whose patina was worth recovering and incorporating into contemporary prose.

El reino de este mundo is about the Haitian Revolution. The collision of the African and European worlds in Haiti allowed Carpentier to posit and practice the theory of "marvelous

American reality," which later would come to be known as "magical realism." In a dramatic scene in which the colonists burn the rebel slave Makandal at the stake, the blacks believe that using his magical powers, he flies away unharmed. But the magic of the novel as text is that it is built on a complex numerological structure involving the dates of the events and even the number of the chapters. It is a scheme that Carpentier claims in the prologue imposed itself on him unconsciously, an instance of the marvelous American reality expressing itself through him. Although he criticizes Surrealism in that prologue, this claim is a vestige of Surrealism. Similar practices and scenes occur in short stories that Carpentier wrote in the period, the 1940s, and which he later collected in *Guerra del tiempo* (*War of Time*, 1958), a book that had great influence in the 1960s among the new novelists and that contains the paradigmatic magical realist stories.

By 1958 Carpentier had published two new novels in which his work had again recast itself: *Los pasos perdidos* (*The Lost Steps*, 1953), and *El acoso* (*Manhunt*, 1956). The first would become his best-known novel, inspiring some critics to call for a Nobel Prize for Carpentier. It is the first-person tale of an intellectual—a composer and musicologist—who travels to the South American jungle in search of some primitive instruments to prove his theory about the origins of music. The most important thing that the narrator-protagonist discovers is that mankind is not one with nature, with the natural cycles that he claimed infused him with the numerological scheme that made up *El reino de este mundo*. That realization leads Carpentier to look for political developments as the foundation of history and the model for narrative. This is what supports the structures of his subsequent novels: *El acoso*, which is the tale of a student activist who betrays his comrades and is hunted and killed, and *El siglo de las luces* (The century of lights, unfortunately translated as *Explosion in a Cathedral*, 1962), in which he returns to the period of the Haitian Revolution but broadens the scope to include much of the Caribbean, France, and Spain.

Carpentier's reinvention of himself during the 1940s was concomitant with his readings of the most influential Latin American writer ever, not so well known at the time, Jorge Luis Borges. Borges made Carpentier rethink the process of writing fiction in the midst of the radical changes that Modernism had brought about. Because he took a turn toward historical fiction, Carpentier did not follow Borges's example, but Borges had made self-reflection and self-awareness of the craft of fiction as the basis of writing, and Carpentier took this to heart. Asturias was still too local and linked to regionalism, while Borges, without abandoning his appreciation of Argentine traditions, was producing stories that reached to the essence of writing itself.

It is good to remember that Borges's most celebrated book, *Ficciones*, appeared in 1944, and that the stories in it had been previously published in journals that Carpentier may have had access to in Havana, and after 1945, in Caracas. All of Latin American fiction is indebted to Borges, and that debt began to accrue early, even before he became known outside Latin America.

Borges started as a poet and was one of the founders of *Ultraísmo*, one of the radical movements of the twenties. Born in Buenos Aires to a family of some distinction, he was a bookish, introverted boy and young man, who had a thorough education at home, in his father's library, in school, and later in Switzerland. In Europe he learned German and French; English he knew from home because his maternal grandmother, who lived with the family, was from England. An avid if selective reader, Borges became, back in Buenos Aires in the thirties, an influential intellectual and writer. He was one of the founders and promoters of *Sur*, one of the most significant journals in Latin American literary history.

Although Borges had left-wing leanings in his early youth, he became increasingly disenchanted with political movements and came to abhor both Fascism and Communism. The publication of *Ficciones* in 1944 and *El Aleph* in 1949 solidified his reputation as one of the leading Argentine and Latin American writers, although, except for France, he was still largely unknown elsewhere. After receiving together with Samuel Beckett the Formentor Prize in 1961, he became one of the most influential modern writers.

There is a Borges world made up of recognizable objects: the library, the labyrinth, mirrors, the encyclopedia, the book. There are also Borgesian themes: the infinite, games, systems, the universe as a book, a programmatic self-effacement, and a recognizable kind of wit, or wisdom, which is preserved not only in his texts but also in a vast repertory of anecdotes. Many are witticisms. Borges liked to deflate clichés, received values, and reputations. There is a Borges style, whose main feature is a passion for brevity and the rejection of rhetoric. His Spanish has the terseness of English. Brevity and concision are also keys to his narrative and his approach to knowledge. The most ambitious theories can be reduced to an encyclopedia entry; he loved encyclopedias, especially the *Britannica*. Borges wrote using startling adjectives, as if the world were made up of secondary qualities, not of essences; many times the adjective is an oxymoron.

There is a Borges "effect" that can be perceived in John Barth, Julio Cortázar, Carpentier, García Márquez, Italo Calvino, Umberto Eco, and in Maurice Blanchot, Michel Foucault, Gerard Genette, and Jacques Derrida. That effect is also projected retrospectively by Borges's particular way of reading classics such as Homer, Dante, and Cervantes. An elegant, playfully ironic skepticism, together with a fondness for the undecidable, enigmas, puzzles, and labyrinths, as well as for minor genres such as the detective story, are the most visible components of Borges's style and thought. Taken together these components suggest theories about writing and reading that John Barth has associated with postmodernism, a literature that is accessible to readers, that does not deny Modernism and its repudiation of nineteenth-century pieties but that transcends it. Postmodernist literature is one that showcases its being fictional and displays its literary make-up. He gives as examples Calvino and García Márquez.

Borges came to world attention in 1961, two years before the publication of Julio Cortázar's *Rayuela* (*Hopscotch*, 1963), which was the book that detonated the Boom of the Latin American novel. Borges would bask in the glare of publicity with Cortázar and the other writers who came to prominence in the sixties, Gabriel García Márquez (Colombia, 1928), Carlos Fuentes (Mexico, 1928), Mario Vargas Llosa (Peru, 1936), and others like José Donoso (Chile, 1924–96), José Lezama Lima (Cuba, 1910–76), and Guillermo Cabrera Infante (Cuba, 1929–2005). An Argentine like Borges, Cortázar (1914–84) had published his first story in *Anales de Buenos Aires*, a journal that the author of *Ficciones* ran in the late forties, and was obviously Borges's disciple. But what Borges did not share with Cortázar and most of the others was their politics, and especially their support of the Cuban Revolution, which had triumphed in 1959 and was one of the chief factors in the elevation to prominence of Latin American literature.

The Cuban Revolution brought attention to Latin America all over a world now connected by the mass media, especially television, as no other event before, including World War II. The image of Fidel Castro speaking to the masses after Fulgencio Batista's flight was instantaneously flashed to all continents. Here was a young, bearded revolutionary who had defeated a regular army with a ragtag group of followers, one of whom, the Argentine Ernesto "Che" Guevara, was as photogenic and quotable as Castro. Both seemed to embody a casual, informal approach to politics and the military that was unheard of in Latin America, where strutting generals in elaborate uniforms were the norm. Castro and his group seemed free from any connections to old political parties like the Communists; they wanted independence for their island republic. Theirs was a nationalist revolution, parallel to efforts in other countries, like Algeria, to break free from the shackles of colonialism. Support for the revolution was nearly universal in Cuba and enthusiastic and multitudinous elsewhere, where it was seen as the spearhead of a worldwide anti-imperialist movement.

The Cuban Revolution seemed like the dawn of a new era, and intellectuals and artists flocked to display their devotion to the cause. Ernest Hemingway, who lived near Havana, seemed to join in the spirit briefly. Jean Paul Sartre soon visited Cuba; Carpentier, who had been living in Caracas since 1945 moved back to Havana, and Neruda visited the island. Very soon García Márquez, Fuentes, and Vargas Llosa did so too. The Cuban capital became the hub of Latin American literature and even of the literature of what came to be known as that of the Third World.

The new regime took advantage of the situation and created cultural institutions to channel the fervor. One was *Lunes de Revolución*, a tabloid published on Mondays by the official newspaper *Revolución* (hence the name), which reached unheard of levels of readership. It published a wide variety of writers from Cuba and around the world. It was directed by Guillermo Cabrera Infante, a rising star who had worked as a film critic for *Carteles*, a popular weekly in the 1950s.

Casa de las Américas, which published an ambitious literary journal by that name was founded to bring together artists and intellectuals from Latin America. It held symposia, gave literary prizes in various categories, and invited to Havana important figures in literature and other arts. (For example, issue 26 of *Casa de las Américas*, from 1964, features work by Alejo Carpentier, Julio Cortázar, Juan Carlos Onetti, Ernesto Sábato, Carlos Fuentes, Mario Vargas Llosa, Juan Goytisolo, Italo Calvino, Alain Robbe-Grillet, and others.) A writers' union was organized, which also offered awards. The Afro-Cuban poet Nicolás Guillén was named its president. All of these activities bore fruit. Havana became the center of Latin American art and literature, parallel to Paris, Barcelona, Buenos Aires, and Mexico City, yet surpassing them all because it combined, as never before, a political as well as an aesthetic comradeship.

As the Castro regime hardened and turned into a dictatorship allied to the Soviet Union, enthusiasm for its cultural policies waned. In 1961 *Lunes de Revolución* was closed at a meeting at the National Library; Castro announced that everything within the revolution was allowed, but nothing against the revolution was permitted. Thousands of alleged homosexuals were sent to concentration camps, among them many artists. The persecution of dissidents began in earnest, as did the flight of writers like Cabrera Infante. In 1967 Heberto Padilla, a poet, won an official prize with his book *Fuera del juego* (*Out of the Game*), but he was reprimanded and later jailed. These actions provoked a critical uproar throughout the intellectual and artistic world, and many broke with Castro. But others, like García Márquez and Cortázar, remained loyal to the regime, as did Carpentier, who had become a cultural advisor to the Cuban diplomatic legation in Paris, a position from which he comfortably observed the disputes and was safe from the deteriorating living conditions in Havana.

Outraged that he was criticized by the cultural commissars in Havana for attending a Pen Club meeting in New York, Neruda distanced himself from the Castro regime and in his memoirs mocked some of its supporters, including Carpentier. The group of young and not so young Cuban writers that emerged after 1959 thinned out with the exile of Severo Sarduy, Reinaldo Arenas, Antonio Benítez Rojo, Padilla, and many others. Lezama Lima lived out his life in his beloved Havana, marginalized by the conformist cultural bureaucracy. After the death of Guillén, the Writers' Union was directed by a series of figures of diminishing stature. But the initial impact of the revolution on Cuban and Latin American literature was deep and lasting, and one of the results was the Boom of the Latin American novel, even though Fuentes and Vargas Llosa broke early with the regime.

Simultaneous with developments in Havana, there appeared in Paris a journal, *Mundo nuevo*, directed by the Uruguayan critic Emir Rodríguez Monegal, that gathered together many of the same writers who were going to Havana and the progressively larger number of those who did not. Vargas Llosa, García Márquez, Ernesto Sábato, Octavio Paz, Clarice Lispector, Sarduy, a brilliant new Argentine novelist Manuel Puig, and many others published in *Mundo nuevo*, a magazine that because of its inclusiveness and high quality, not to mention that its seat was Paris, was instrumental in the promotion of the "nueva novela" or "new novel," as the emerging movement was called. *Mundo nuevo* also published poets such as Paz, as well as the Uruguayan Juana de Ibarbourou, the Mexican Homero Aridjis, the Venezuelan Guillermo Sucre, and the Chilean Nicanor Parra.

The booming Latin American novel was accompanied by a group of excellent poets. In the contentious spirit of the cold war, and motivated by envy because *Mundo nuevo* was stealing its thunder, the Cuban cultural bureaucracy accused *Mundo nuevo* of receiving funds from the CIA (as if the Cuban regime were not being financed by the Soviets). The journal was supported by American foundations that may have received some funds from the CIA, but the journal did not discriminate on the basis of politics when it came to deciding whom to publish. Pablo Neruda and Ernesto Cardenal contributed poems, the first a notorious Communist, the second would become a pillar of Sandinismo in Nicaragua. *Mundo nuevo*, because of the literature and criticism it published, including that of its director, is a high watermark in Latin American literature and was a decisive vehicle in the emergence and development of the new Latin American novel.

Born in Brussels of Argentine parents but raised in Argentina, where he studied to be a teacher, Cortázar lived in Paris from 1952 until his death, working in the translation department of UNESCO. His Belgian childhood and long years in Paris left him speaking Spanish with a guttural French "r." A gentle giant, six and a half feet tall, Cortázar was predominantly a short-story writer. Before 1963, when he published *Rayuela* (Hopscotch), he was already the author of three story collections, *Bestiario* (*Bestiary*, 1951), *Final del juego* (*End of the Game*, 1956), and *Las armas secretas* (*Secret Weapons*). More than Borges, Cortázar was drawn by instances of the fantastic and uncanny. His characters tend to be young people, often in Europe, who face amazing situations, like the one who goes to the Paris aquarium to look intensely at an axolotl (Mexican salamander) only to become or discover that he is one; another begins to vomit bunny rabbits. A cosmopolitan polyglot, Cortázar easily blended in with the counterculture of the sixties when he became famous and joined left-wing causes with more enthusiasm than thoughtfulness.

Rayuela was an instant hit and best seller, whose translation into English by Gregory Rabassa won the National Book Award in 1966. It is a huge novel of more than six hundred pages, foreboding at first. But it comes equipped with a "Table of Instructions" giving the reader several options about the order in which to read the book, and how many of the 155 chapters to read, a good number of which are declared to be "expendable." Cortázar himself referred to it as an "antinovel."

As its title indicates, *Rayuela* is like a game, a playful work made up of brief chapters, often consisting of newspaper articles, such as the one from London's *Observer* about the dangers for boys of catching their foreskins in the zippers of their pants. A few consist of quotations from other writers. One is completely written in gibberish. Some chapters contain the ruminations of one Morelli about literature; he represents the author within the novel, though Horacio Olivera, the protagonist, is also a writer. The expendable chapters furnish details about the main plot, which is ultimately very traditional. It involves Horacio's quest for Lucía, known as La Maga, his lover, a strange woman he loves and who represents truth. The first sentence of the novel is: "¿Encontraría a la Maga?" (Would I find La Maga?). Both belong to a group of young people, the Club, who are not so young any more, living in Paris.

The novel is divided into three parts, "Del lado de allá" (the other side), which is Paris, "Del lado de acá" (this side), which is Buenos Aires; and "De otros lados" (other sides), which contains the expendable chapters. Horacio returns to Buenos Aires, where he meets his old friend Traveler who, despite his name, never travels. He has married Talita and lives a conventional life working in the administration of a circus. But the circus owner sells it to buy a mental institution, to which they all move. Horacio has rediscovered his obsessive love for La Maga, whom he now confuses with Talita, creating a tense triangle with his friend. In one scene Horacio thinks he sees La Maga playing hopscotch in the yard, but it is Talita. The game of hopscotch, with its various squares that the player must visit after throwing his markers on his way to the last one, sometimes called "cielo" or "heaven" is an apt (perhaps too much so) representation of the "game of life," thus a good symbol for Horacio's quest. He begins to build an elaborate if precarious defense, a flimsy barricade, against Traveler, whom he fears will come after him. In the end Horacio builds a precarious bridge between buildings from which he intends to jump to commit suicide. But the novel ends without the reader knowing for sure if he does so.

Like the underlying plot of *Rayuela*, a conventional quest romance, Cortázar's concerns are the same as those of other Argentine writers, like Eduardo Mallea and Ernesto Sábato, not to mention all the Latin American writers who quested for identity in their essays, poems, stories, and novels. Perhaps what *Rayuela* proposes is that playfulness and humor are essential to interpret the most pressing issues of the human condition. That being the case, *Rayuela* deserves, like the *Quijote*, a very important place in literary history, though in truth its fame has diminished with the passing years, and Cortázar is now mostly admired for his short stories.

In the 1950s, García Márquez also spent his season in Paris, working as a correspondent for Colombian newspapers, who paid him little and sporadically. Born in the small Colombian town of Aracataca, García Márquez abandoned his law studies early to become a bohemian journalist and writer, living for a time in

Cartagena, on the Caribbean coast of Colombia that he seems to prefer. He published two novels, *La hojarasca* (*The Leaf Storm*, 1955) and *La mala hora* (*In Evil Hour*, 1962), and a novella, *El coronel no tiene quien le escriba* (*No One Writes to the Colonel*, 1961) before his masterpiece *Cien años de soledad* (*One Hundred Years of Solitude*, 1967). The early novels have gained importance retrospectively but are run of the mill; the novella was excellent and introduced the town of Macondo, which would be the famous setting of *Cien años de soledad.* In the interim García Márquez had been to Cuba, and he worked in New York as a correspondent for the Castro regime news agency, Prensa Latina. García Márquez's bond with Castro has lasted until today, having now exceeded fifty years of servitude.

The Nobel Prize he received in 1982 turned him into an international celebrity, a star who could afford to have apartments or houses in Paris, Mexico City, and Havana (provided by the grateful regime). He continued to produce, publishing *El otoño del patriarca* (*The Autumn of the Patriarch*) in 1975, a dictator novel, *Crónica de una muerte anunciada* (*Chronicle of a Death Foretold*) in 1981, a novella, and the ambitious *El amor en los tiempos del cólera* (*Love in the Time of Cholera*) in 1985. In 1989 *El general en su laberinto* (*The General in His Labyrinth*), about Simón Bolívar, appeared, and in 1994 *Del amor y otros demonios* (*Of Love and Other Demons*), both well received. His journalistic exercise *Noticia de un secuestro* (*News of a Kidnapping*, 1996), about the dreadful political situation in Colombia, was not as well liked, and he has been criticized for his tale of senile love *Memoria de mis putas tristes* (*Memories of My Melancholy Whores*), published in 2004. The last does seem to reveal a decline in García Márquez's creative power.

Cien años de soledad is the hundred-year saga of the Buendía family in the town they founded, Macondo, in the midst of the jungle. While the historical events surrounding Macondo—civil wars, exploitation by the United Fruit Company, the massacre of banana workers who go on strike—is verifiably Colombian, the town's history is like a synthesis of all Latin American history, from the discovery and conquest by the Spanish until the early twentieth century. It might even be argued that, because time begins before things have names in a setting that is paradisiacal, and an original sin of sorts sets off the family's history, the story of Macondo is that of mankind. There is an Old Testament air about those patriarchs who father numerous and intricate families and lead their peoples through the wilderness.

One of the many virtues of the novel is how García Márquez combines these vast, legend-like, and potentially allegorical or mythical tales with the minute, particular passing of time and the unfolding of daily life in the home of the Buendías and the ordinary activities of Macondo. Another is the tone of the narrator, who seems to tell the story from within the world of the characters, with their traditional beliefs in the existence of the supernatural. It is a tone in which hyperbole prevails as a hint of irony because people, things, and events cannot be that large, that many, or last that long. In that regard, this is a very funny novel. Another ironic twist is the overtly literary character of certain events, characters, and allusions, and the discretely but powerfully constructed nature of the whole fictional world, a tightly woven construct that seems to be the work of a watchmaker or jeweler. It is as if Borges, instead of writing the short story "Tlön, Uqbar, Orbis Tertius," had written a true regionalist novel, not a parody.

Fuentes, of all of the Boom writers, is the most cosmopolitan. The son of a diplomat, he was not born in Mexico, but in Panama. He grew up in Washington, D.C., and in Santiago, Chile, and studied at the University of Mexico and in Geneva. He speaks English like an American and is fluent in French. Active in Mexico's complicated political world, he has been a diplomat (ambassador to France), and a polemical commentator on national and international events. He has been intensively concerned with the issue of Mexican identity, both in his fiction and in his considerable essayistic and journalistic production. Fuentes was indelibly influenced by Paz's *El laberinto de la soledad* in his early work, and he has been a follower of artistic, philosophical, and critical trends throughout his career.

French thinkers like Michel Foucault and Jacques Derrida enthralled him at some point, as did the Spanish cultural historian Américo Castro, whose theories about the important role played by Arabic and Jewish cultures in Spanish history he followed, particularly in his writings about Cervantes. Fuentes has always been anxiously *au courant* and has cultivated celebrities in politics and the arts. Like Vargas Llosa and García Márquez, he was an early supporter of the Cuban Revolution, spent time in Havana, and learned much from Carpentier, whose work left an imprint on Fuentes's best-known novel, *La muerte de Artemio Cruz* (*The Death of Artemio Cruz*, 1962). He broke with Castro following the Padilla affair mentioned earlier. *Aura*, a novel also published in 1962, follows Henry James's *The Aspern Papers* and is one of Fuentes's best works.

La muerte de Artemio Cruz follows the structure of Carpentier's story "Viaje a la semilla" (Journey Back to the Source). It is told backwards, from Artemio's deathbed to his birth. He is an immensely powerful and wealthy man who has profited in the aftermath of the Mexican Revolution through guile and arm-twisting. A combatant in the revolution, he has used his influence to cajole others in doing his bidding, controlling newspapers, finances, and the corrupt politics of the postrevolutionary period. One of Fuentes's models for the novel is Orson Welles's film classic *Citizen Kane*, which is based on the life of newspaper tycoon William Randolph Hearst. But Fuentes has added the innovation of having the story told by three voices, Artemio's "I," "you," and "he," as if they were a drama within his conscience, first as he lays dying (another model is Faulkner's novel by that title), and later in key episodes of his life. At the time, in Spanish, this was quite a startling technique, and it is effective in the portrayal of the protagonist from several perspectives. Fuentes's novel anteceded Cortázar's *Rayuela* by one year, but it was not quite as scandalous in theme or method and did not provoke as great a reaction as the Argentine's. But *La muerte de Artemio Cruz* did have a very recognizable subject in Latin American terms: the Mexican Revolution. It was a novel that followed in the tradition of Guzmán, Azuela, and Rulfo, and it appeared at a time when the topic of revolution was in the air because of Cuba.

Though he published other novels before *Terra Nostra* (1975), like *Cambio de piel* (*A Change of Skin*, 1967), *Zona sagrada* (*Holy Place*, 1967), and *Cumpleaños* (*Birthday*, 1969), the massive *Terra Nostra* was Fuentes's most ambitious project in the 1970s and perhaps of his entire career. The novel is a probe into Hispanic culture through three of its principal literary myths: Don Quijote, Don Juan, and Celestina. In a way, Fuentes is following a system similar to that of Giambattista Vico by approaching a culture through the stories it has created. There are other legendary characters, like Philip II; Antonio Pérez, the traitor; Guzmán de Alfarache, the rogue; and even the unnamed shipwreck victim in Góngora's *Soledades*. *Terra Nostra* attempts to be a summa. Cervantes is the chronicler who will morph into Carlos Fuentes, no less, and Philip II will become Francisco Franco. Each of these seminal figures will produce images of themselves in the future. They all speak in their "own" voices. Toward the end, characters from contemporary Latin American novels appear.

The ideological underpinning is Américo Castro's theories about Spanish culture being divided against itself because of the caste struggle provoked by friction among the three religions present in the Peninsula during the Middle Ages. That conflict is imperfectly resolved by the Catholic Kings, who defeat the Moors at Granada and expel the Jews, just as the New World is being discovered by Columbus. The New World will be a grandiose repetition of the Old, with all its defects and discord.

The youngest of the principal writers of the Boom was Vargas Llosa. He was raised in Bolivia and in his native rural Peru, an experience that would be reflected in several of his major novels. He moved to Lima as a young man, where he studied under the historian Raúl Porras Barrenechea, and began working as a journalist. He soon distinguished himself as a short-story writer, winning a literary prize that sent him to Paris. He was fascinated by the French capital and its intellectual and artistic debates. It was the 1950s, and Sartre and Camus were the principal voices heard. In 1962, when he was only twenty-two, Vargas Llosa won the coveted Seix Barral Prize with his first novel, *La ciudad y los perros* (The city and the dogs, translated as *The Time of the Hero*). Set in a military school in Lima, the novel tells the story of sadistic quarrels among the students, the bullying of the weaker ones, and the corrupt authoritarianism bred in such an institution. It was rightly interpreted as a critique of the Peruvian military establishment, and Vargas Llosa prudently remained in Europe, except for visits to revolutionary Cuba.

In 1965 he published an even more daring and ambitious novel, *La casa verde* (*The Green House*), named after the whorehouse in which much of the novel takes place. Bonifacia, who is about to become a nun, is transformed into "La Selvática," or the Jungle Native, the most notorious prostitute in the Casa Verde. In 1967, the novel won the first Rómulo Gallegos Prize in Venezuela, an award that became very prestigious and would be won later by García Márquez and Fuentes. Vargas Llosa, who was not only being published in *Mundo nuevo* but written about admiringly by its director Rodríguez Monegal, was being buoyed by the loudest bangs of the Boom. It was about this time that he, along with many others writers and intellectuals, broke with the Castro regime. He would become in the future its persistent critic and adversary.

After his successes in the 1960s and 1970s, Vargas Llosa's production continued unabated. A recent success was his *La fiesta del chivo* (*The Feast of the Goat*, 2000) about Trujillo's dictatorship

6. Mario Vargas Llosa of Peru won the Nobel Prize in 2010.

in the Dominican Republic, but this is but one among many. He is a prolific, fluent, and original storyteller in the manner of Balzac and Pérez Galdós, and the variety of novels that he has published is astonishing, from *La tía Julia y el escribidor* (*Aunt Julia and the Scriptwriter*, 1977), a hilarious novel about a writer of soap operas who mixes the plots of the several stories he is writing, to *La guerra del fin del mundo* (*The War of the End of the World*, 1981), a retelling of the Canudos incidents in nineteenth-century Brazil, in which a band of religious fanatics build a city and the government tries to dislodge them: it is a story told in the Brazilian classic *Os sertoes* (*Rebellion in the Backlands*, 1902) by Euclides da Cunha. This may be Vargas Llosa's masterpiece. It is a symphonic novel in which he includes da Cunha as a character, and in which his familiar concerns about violence, heroism, and guilt resurface. In 2010, Vargas Llosa was awarded a long-deserved Nobel Prize.

A less visible member of the Boom club was the Chilean José Donoso (1924–96). Educated partially at Princeton and involved with the Iowa Writers' Workshop, Donoso spoke English and was steeped in American fiction. His first stories, in fact, were written in English. His best-known novels are *Coronación* (*Coronation*, 1957), *El lugar sin límites* (*Hell Has No Limits*, 1967), and *El obsceno pájaro de la noche* (*The Obscene Bird of Night*, 1970). He also wrote a history of the Boom, *Historia personal del Boom* (*The Boom in Spanish American Literature: A Personal History*, 1977). *Coronación*, which antedates the Boom, is a very Jamesian novel about the Chilean bourgeoisie with touches of the grotesque, a Donoso trait.

El lugar sin límites takes place in a brothel. It is the story of an enormously endowed homosexual who impregnates a whore. *El obsceno pájaro de la noche* is the most experimental, difficult, and disconcerting of Donoso's novels, dealing essentially with madness and the loss of identity. It is a massive novel that Donoso claimed almost cost him his own sanity. The best description of its fictional world is the Indian myth of *imbunche*, which appears in the novel, in which the victim is monstrously transformed by closing off all of his body's orifices. Donoso's fiction is equally sealed off and self-contained, a hallucinatory kind of microcosm. But it was his gift to be able to create such an airless environment without its existing in a vacuum. An exile in Mexico, the United States, and Spain for most of his life, and a critic of the Pinochet dictatorship, Donoso returned to Chile at the end.

An even less visible associate of the Boom was the Cuban José Lezama Lima (1910–76). Lezama was a poet and the least cosmopolitan writer imaginable, although his erudition was immense. In contrast to the Boom writers, he was known for not traveling abroad and having only Spanish as a language of culture. Yet his novel *Paradiso* (*Paradiso*), published in 1966, caused a scandal as well as widespread astonishment and admiration. The scandal was provoked by the explicit description of homosexual acts, which, together with Lezama's indifference to the Castro regime, led to having half the print run confiscated by the authorities. Surprise and approval came precisely because of the frankness with which homosexuality was dealt with, and because of the truly shocking originality of the work. Cortázar expressed his admiration in a widely disseminated essay.

Lezama's novel is a protracted *bildungsroman*, reminiscent of Joyce's *Portrait of the Artist as a Young Man*, but richer, and more like *Ulysses* in its minute depiction of Havana and in the language Lezama uses, which is exactly like that of his poetry: dense, allusive, oblivious to grammar, and rhetorical registers. *Paradiso* is a profound work that invents its own discourse and responds to the deepest issues in the human condition. Because of Lezama's reluctance to travel, added to denials of permission to leave Cuba by the Castro regime, and the strangeness of his work, which is not reducible to the conventionalities of Modernism, *Paradiso* did not become as popular as works by García Márquez, Fuentes, or Vargas Llosa. But the writers knew that in him they were facing a master who may very well have outdone them all, working from his modest home in old Havana.

A different kind of Boom fellow-traveler was the Cuban Guillermo Cabrera Infante (1929–2005), best known for his hilarious and highly experimental novel *Tres tristes tigres* (translated as *Three Trapped Tigers*, 1966) and for his persistent opposition to the Castro regime, with which he was associated in the early years. The novel is Joycean in its use of monologues, variations of Havana speech, and protracted discussions among the characters, young men and women trying to make it in the prosperous media and showbiz environment of the Cuban capital in the late fifties. It also shows features derived from Cortázar's *Rayuela*.

It is a novel rife with social melodrama; most of the characters are poor, some mulattoes or blacks, and from the provinces, all desperately transforming themselves to pass as sophisticated and talented. One of them, dead by the time the novel begins, Bustrofedon, has an uncanny ability to play with language, and the others are in possession of audio tapes in which he parodies well-known Cuban writers as if they were narrating the death of Trotsky. The parodies are brilliant and the constant language games throughout the book dazzling. It is, moreover, a novel that begins with the emcee at the Tropicana Nightclub introducing some of the characters who later will appear in the fiction; hence the whole of it is to be taken as a nightclub act, a show: the world is a stage. Cabrera Infante was among the younger writers who published in *Mundo nuevo*. He lived in London for many years, and died there, a very bitter exile rightfully obsessed by the fate of his country.

A first generation of younger novelists, still associated with the Boom, was led by the Cuban Severo Sarduy (1937–93) and the Argentinian Manuel Puig (1932–80). Like Cabrera Infante they were both published in *Mundo nuevo*. Sarduy produced highly experimental novels that were, in many ways, parodies of those written by the novelists of the Boom. In Paris since 1960, he was among the first Cuban writers to flee the Castro regime. In the French capital he was associated with the *Tel Quel* group. This was the journal around which gathered the Structuralist and post-Structuralist groups. Sarduy was the only Latin American intellectual to be really immersed in *Tel Quel*'s work, though they had an influence on the likes of Paz and Fuentes. His adherence to their theories made him difficult to read, but he was extremely original and deep. His *De donde son los cantantes* (translated as *From Cuba with a Song*, 1967), and especially *Maitreya* (1978), are minor masterpieces that will never have a readership as wide as that of books by García Márquez or Fuentes, but because of their originality, they will remain as important works in the history of Latin American literature.

Puig's obsession was the impact of the mass media, particularly film, on ordinary people and therefore on literature. His *La traición de Rita Hayworth* (*Betrayed by Rita Hayworth*, 1968), set in a small, fictitious Argentine town, has much in common with the work of the boom writers and is just as good. *El beso de la mujer araña* (*The Kiss of the Spiderwoman*) was something fresh and a masterpiece in its own right. It is the story of a political activist and a homosexual confined to the same jail cell in Argentina, with the latter seducing the former by telling him the plots of films he has seen. Although highly original, Puig is refreshingly unself-conscious and easy to read. This book was turned into an excellent movie. The early death from AIDS of Sarduy and Puig, two accomplished yet still promising writers, made a smooth transition from the Boom to a new generation of novelists impossible. Another early death of the same disease was that of Reinaldo Arenas (Cuba, 1943–90), a truly gifted writer who had suffered relentless harassment by the Castro regime until he escaped during the Mariel boatlift and left enduring works like *El mundo alucinante* (*Hallucinations*, 1966), a retelling of the life of Fray Servando Teresa de Mier, a Mexican priest (1765–1827) who called for independence and was persecuted relentlessly. Arenas also published a gripping memoir, *Antes que anochezca* (*Before Night Falls*, 1992), which became a successful film.

Chapter 6
Latin American literature today

The emergence of such a clear-cut historical movement as the Boom of the Latin American novel, which was accompanied by a parallel one in poetry if we consider that Pablo Neruda, Octavio Paz, José Lezama Lima, Jorge Luis Borges, and Nicanor Parra were active in the period, inevitably provoked the desire to discern the appearance of another break, particularly one that decisively closed off such a recognizable era. If there was a Boom, then there had to be a post-Boom. But in literary history it is very difficult to distinguish breaks from continuities unless truly major works and writers arise, as with the Boom, and no new figures of the stature of the Boom writers have appeared, and no poets like those mentioned have come forward.

Major writers are a rarity, even if the advent of several at once makes one expect the next group to promptly rise above the horizon. On the whole, Latin American literature—though active and producing many works of quality—is not today what it was in the last three decades of the twentieth century. The death of Paz in 1996 may very well have meant the end of an era.

In the 1980s, a deliberately post-Boom literary movement that attempted to distance itself from magical realism and the Modernist aesthetics of the Boom novelists emerged, dubbing itself "MacOndo," an irreverent takeoff on the name of the town in

Cien años de soledad, Macondo. The writers involved portrayed a Latin America that is urban, globalized, and overwhelmed by U.S. culture, such as McDonald's restaurants. A similar group, mostly Mexican, called itself "Nueva Onda," "New Wave," and opposed not only Fuentes but also Paz and his hegemonic literary group. Neither of these groups produced works of enduring value or a compelling literary figure of national—much less international—acclaim. Macondo, like Homer's Ithaca, Virgil's Rome, Balzac's Paris, or Dickens's London, cannot be denied its place in literary history.

Gathered in two groups, the newer Latin American writers clearly opposed the Boom: MacOndo and the Crack. MacOndo was in fact the title of a short-story anthology edited by the Chilean writers Alberto Fuguet and Sergio Gómez in 1996. In that same year a group of Mexicans published the "Crack Manifesto." They rejected the exoticism they perceived in followers of García Márquez, who portrayed a rural Latin America that Europeans and Americans wanted to read about made up of ghostly towns, ruled by outrageous military dictators, and rife with improbable happenings attributed to local magical practices.

The new writers favored instead an image of Latin America as the product of globalization. They wrote realist stories and novels with urban settings that were heavily influenced by the media. These writers may have been part of a veritable paradigm shift. It is true that the Boom writers, heirs to Modernism, were deeply and centrally concerned with the issue of Latin American identity, which they sought through their experiments with language and probes into history. The new writers claim not to be preoccupied by the issue of cultural identity, but of individual identity in a world shot through with the alienating images with which film, television, and advertising bombard them.

The French philosopher François Lyotard spoke in *La Condition postmoderne: rapport sur le savoir* (*The Postmodern Condition: A*

Report on Knowledge, 1979) of the collapse of the grand narratives like Marxism, philosophical doctrines that offered an all-encompassing view of the world and of history. These doctrines, derived from the Enlightenment but in my view ultimately stemming from Christianity, provided the novel with a large context for its own narrative. Identity was a grand, comprehensive narrative in Latin American literature, but by the time the work of Severo Sarduy appeared it had already been shattered, and he wrote about constellations of its shards.

The collapse of the Berlin Wall and the implosion of the Soviet Union marked the downfall of Communism, the historical version (or perversion) of one of those narratives. In Latin America Marxism has been, and in many places persists in being, a secular religion in spite of the failure of Communism. Perhaps the so-called post-Boom, if it does exist, is an expression of this postmodern condition. The feeling now is that the world cannot be changed by literature or by the intellectuals, whereas before, utopia was a palpable thing, available in places like Cuba.

Movements like MacOndo and the Crack reified and distorted the Boom in their competitive zeal. García Márquez may very well have been the most influential writer, but there were others, like Fuentes, Cortázar, Vargas Llosa, Donoso, and more recently Puig and Sarduy, who were already reflecting some of the realities of contemporary Latin America that these movements mention. A larger problem for the new writers is that while rebellions against authority make good journalistic copy and sound bites, they have to be accompanied by significant literary works to have a lasting impact, and none of those involved in MacOndo or the Crack has yet published a work that comes close to *Cien años de soledad* in terms of quality or reception.

Two of them, however, have achieved some recognition for meritorious books and stories. Associated with MacOndo, the Bolivian Edmundo Paz Soldán (1967) has published, among other novels, *El delirio de Turing* (*Turing's Obsession*, 2003), a complex but readable story about a cryptographer and hackers in a Bolivia under dictatorial rule. It is a fresh topic. Paz Soldán seems to be keenly interested in riddles: one of his best short stories, one of the finest from Latin America in the past thirty years, is about a man whose job is to compose crossword puzzles. Jorge Volpi (Mexico, 1968), was associated with the Crack. He has published a few well-received novels. One, *El fin de la locura* (*End of the Madness*, 2003), deals with Paris during the post-Structuralist sixties. It is a satire and a deconstruction, particularly of French psychoanalyst Jacques Lacan and his gullible Latin American followers. It is also indirectly a good final assessment of the Boom. *En busca de Klingsor* (*In Search of Klingsor*, 1999), which won the Biblioteca Breve Prize in Spain, deals with the pursuit of the atom bomb by German scientists during World War II.

Two women from the Boom years, Luisa Valenzuela (Argentina, 1938) and Isabel Allende (Chile, 1942, but born in Lima, Peru) have steadily continued producing work that has been acknowledged in some quarters. Allende, in particular, is very popular in Europe. In her early work she was a very close follower of García Márquez, especially in her novel *La casa de los espíritus* (*The House of Spirits*, 1985). Her work regularly appears in English translation. The daughter of writer Luisa Mercedes Levinson, Valenzuela was raised in a literary household in Buenos Aires and began to write at an early age. She has published novels against the rule of the military in Argentina from a feminist perspective that questions typically Latin American patriarchal attitudes. These include her 1982 collection of short stories *Cambio de armas* (*Change of Guard*), and in 1983 *Cola de lagartija* (*The Lizard's Tail*). She has not fared as well as Allende in English or in Europe, but her work has generated interesting academic criticism.

The essay is flourishing anew, particularly in the work of two exiled Cuban writers, Antonio José Ponte (Cuba, 1964) and Rafael Rojas (Cuba, 1965). Ponte, who also writes poetry and fiction, has published highly original essays, like *La fiesta vigilada* (The Guarded Fiesta, 2007), which in part chronicles the visit of an Italian photographer to Cuba. The essay deals with the progressive decay of Havana under the Castro dictatorship and the construction of architecturally innovative buildings that are never finished or used and become instant ruins. Ponte has an ironic, smooth prose and a sharp eye for details, as when he describes a decrepit jukebox in an old bar that is being refurbished to receive tourists; or his deadpan report of a visit to a museum in which state security displays items from its long history of repression. *La fiesta vigilada* reads like a novel. Rojas, a historian by profession, is a very prolific essayist who has won two prestigious prizes for books on Cuba. In *Tumbas sin sosiego* (Graves without Rest, 2006), he draws a balance of revisionist versions of Cuban history by intellectuals allied with Castro. It is a well-researched book that, because it is written with the balanced approach of a historian, is a devastating indictment of some of the more prominent government intellectuals and their predecessors.

Rojas and Ponte, along with writers from Latin America and Spain, publish their work in a journal, *Letras libres*, which is the heir to all the great Latin American literary magazines from the past. Based in Mexico City, where it is directed by the distinguished historian Enrique Krauze, who had been involved with Octavio Paz in publishing *Vuelta*, *Letras libres* also brings out each issue, slightly different, in Madrid. It includes cultural and political commentary, reviews of current books, as well as fiction and poetry. It is the most important cultural Latin American publication of the moment. Cuba's venerable *Casa de las Américas* still comes out, but it lost its influence long ago.

Two writers who have brought Latin American literature back to a place of prominence are the novelists Fernando Vallejo (Colombia, 1942) and Roberto Bolaño (Chile, 1953–2003). Vallejo was born in Medellín, which he left early. He studied philosophy, but later finished a degree in biology. In Rome he studied cinematography and later returned to Colombia to produce films, but he had difficulties with the Colombian government and moved to Mexico in 1971. He still lives there and has taken Mexican citizenship. Vallejo's interests, which are reflected in his fiction and films, are drugs, homosexuality, violence, grammar, and religion. He is openly gay, flamboyant, and a lover of animals, particularly dogs. All of these elements intersect in his most accomplished novel, *La virgen de los sicarios* (*The Lady of the Assassins*, 1994), which is a fictionalized account of his return to Medellín. The narrator-protagonist is a middle-aged homosexual, author of grammar textbooks, who has consecutive relationships with two very young men, teenagers, who work as killers for rival drug cartels. In deadpan style, Vallejo describes the lives of these killers for hire who wind up being killers for pleasure and shoot people dead in the streets at the slightest provocation, real or imagined.

The language of the novel and its title reveal a religious substratum that filters through, as when the boys call the bullet-hole on the foreheads of victims "cross of ashes," like the one Catholics have stamped on their foreheads on Ash Wednesday. The grammarian expresses his love for these boys in lyrical terms, tinged with his knowledge of classical Spanish poetry. *La virgen de los sicarios* is a powerful, pitiless novel, not only because of the sordid, violent ambience that it describes but also because it seems to delve deeply into the worst perversions of the human soul. There is no reprieve in this fiction that reads as if Nietzsche had turned novelist.

In 2003 Vallejo was awarded the Rómulo Gallegos Prize in Caracas, the same honor that had been bestowed on García Márquez, Fuentes, and Vargas Llosa, among other notables. At the ceremony, in protest against prevailing political conditions in Venezuela under Hugo Chávez, he gave a scandalous speech in which he mockingly compared Fidel Castro to Jesus Christ, and he donated the prize money to a society for the protection of animals. Vallejo was subsequently expelled from the country. He provoked another scandal when, upon taking Mexican citizenship, he wrote an outrageous letter explaining why he was renouncing his Colombian citizenship. Vallejo's attitudes and actions seem like a throwback to Decadentism and the *poètes maudits* (Baudelaire, Verlaine, and Rimbaud) that he avowedly admires. Against the background of the pious politically committed and politically correct writers of the Boom and after, Vallejo's stance is a fresh one in every sense of the word.

Bolaño, who is the only recent Latin American writer to have become a celebrity comparable to the Boom writers, had the misfortune of dying at age fifty, when his fame was on the rise and his work was peaking. Posthumously, his reputation has remained very high for a very good reason: the quality of his work.

The son of a truck driver who dropped out of high school to write poetry, Bolaño moved to Mexico while still very young and joined a group of rebellious poets who formed a gang of literary terrorists who shouted at the poetry readings by the élite writers. Their bête noire was Octavio Paz. He would immortalize these young poets in the novel that made him famous, *Los detectives salvajes* (*The Savage Detectives*, 1998), for which he received the Rómulo Gallegos Prize in 1999. By that time Bolaño had settled in Barcelona and had recovered from a heroin addiction he had picked up in his bohemian travels through Europe. The novel was compared to the best by the writers of the Boom and to *Paradiso* by Lezama Lima (Bolaño despised García Márquez and anything that smacked of magical realism). The group activities, narrated by many narrators and centering on the aptly named Ulises Lima, has echoes of the club in *Rayuela*, and Bolaño, who admired Cortázar, was also a follower of the Surrealists and shared other tastes with the Argentine.

Fearing that liver disease would kill him, Bolaño wrote furiously during his last years, concerned about the fate of the two children he had from his Catalonian wife. The new novels were not as lengthy as *Los detectives salvajes*, but they continued to be just as ambitious. *Nocturno de Chile* (Chile nocturne, but translated as *By Night in Chile*, 2000) is a minor masterpiece; less than two hundred pages long, its narrator-protagonist is a dying Chilean priest who recounts his life. A tremendously cultured man who masters the Latin and Greek classics, the priest, who at one point serves as tutor to General Augusto Pinochet and his associates, travels from church to church in Europe helping eradicate the pigeons that rain droppings on them. The solution found by each church, the deployment of falcons, each with a name appropriate to the language and culture of where the church sits, is hilarious and fraught with all kinds of symbolic possibilities. Bolaño has the rare ability of being funny and deep at the same time, and his take on the Catholic Church can be called reverentially satiric. He shows, through his priest, that he knows his Dante, perhaps as well as Jorge Luis Borges, his literary hero.

Will another Bolaño emerge in the near future? There are many literary journals in Latin America, groups of writers gather in the various capitals to discuss their works, and artists and intellectuals from all the Spanish-speaking countries still meet in Paris, Madrid, New York, and other cities around the world for the same reasons (political persecution, yearning for new horizons). In their own countries, even in provincial towns, aspiring novelists and poets sit around café tables to exchange ideas and read each others' texts. A new Bolaño may already exist among them, only waiting to be discovered. Or, better yet, a writer unlike Bolaño, but as original as he was when he appeared on the scene, may surprise all with a work of enduring quality. It is impossible to predict. The patterns of literary history are only noticeable retrospectively.

Further reading

Primary sources

For the texts mentioned or discussed in all chapters, the best source is *The Borzoi Anthology of Latin American Literature* (New York: Knopf, 1977), in two volumes, edited by Emir Rodríguez Monegal. It also covers the colonial period. Modern poetry, from the late nineteenth century (Modernismo) until the end of the twentieth may be read in *Twentieth-Century Latin American Poetry: A Bilingual Anthology*, edited by Stephen Tapscott (Austin: University of Texas Press, 1996). These books should suffice for chapters 1, 2, 4, and 5. A translation of a major modern poet that can be consulted is Pablo Neruda, *Canto General*, trans. Jack Schmitt, introduction by Roberto González Echevarría (Berkeley: University of California Press, 1991).

Most of the authors discussed in chapter 3 also appear in *The Borzoi Anthology*, but the following may be added:

    Gómez de Avellaneda, Gertrudis. *Sab* and *Autobiography*. Translated by Nina M. Scott. Austin: University of Texas Press, 1993.

    Rodó, José Enrique. *Ariel.* Translated by Margaret Sayers Peden. Austin: University of Texas Press, 1988.

    Sarmiento, Domingo Faustino. *Facundo: Civilization and Barbarism.* Translated by Kathleen Ross. Introduction by Roberto González Echevarría. Berkeley: University of California Press, 2003.

Villaverde, Cirilo. *Cecilia Valdés*. Translated by Helen Lane and
Sibylle Fischer. New York: Oxford University Press, 2005.

Fragments of the novels commented upon, as well as short stories,
are also included in *The Borzoi Anthology* and in *The Oxford Book of
Latin American Short Stories*, ed. Roberto González Echevarría (New
York: Oxford University Press, 1997). The following may be added:

Borges, Jorge Luis. *Collected Fictions*. Translated by Andrew
Hurley. New York: Viking, 1998.

Carpentier, Alejo. *The Kingdom of This World*. Translated by
Harriet de Onís. New York: Knopf, 1957.

Fuentes, Carlos. *The Death of Artemio Cruz*. Translated by Sam
Hileman. New York: Farrar, Straus and Giroux, 1964.

Gallegos, Rómulo. *Doña Barbara*. Translated by Robert Malloy.
New York: Peter Smith, 1948.

García Márquez, Gabriel. *One Hundred Years of Solitude*.
Translated by Gregory Rabassa. New York: Harper and Row,
1970.

Lezama Lima, José. *Paradiso*. Translated by Gregory Rabassa. New
York: Farrar, Straus and Giroux, 1974.

Rulfo, Juan. *Pedro Páramo*. Translated by Margaret Sayers Peden.
New York: Grove Press, 1994.

Vargas Llosa, Mario. *Time of the Hero*. Translated by Lysander
Kemp. New York: Grove Press, 1966.

The best two contemporary novelists, Fernando Vallejo and
Roberto Bolaño, who are discussed in chapter 6, may be read in
the following editions:

Bolaño, Roberto. *By Night in Chile*. Translated by Chris Andrews.
New York: New Directions Books, 2003.

Vallejo, Fernando. *Our Lady of the Assassins*. Translated by Paul
Hammond. London: Serpent's Tail, 2001.

Secondary sources

The best source of information about Latin American literature
is *The Handbook of Latin American Studies*, coordinated by the
Library of Congress. It is an annotated bibliography, updated
weekly online at http://lcweb2.loc.gov/hlas/hlashome.html.

A print edition is published by the University of Texas Press. Each year, the coverage of the print edition's new volume alternates between humanities and social sciences. The humanities bibliographies cover both literature and criticism.

Adorno, Rolena. *The Polemics of Possession in Spanish American Narrative*. New Haven, CT: Yale University Press, 2007.

Anderson Imbert, Enrique. *Spanish-American Literature: A History*. Detroit: Wayne State University Press, 1963.

Bloom, Harold, ed. *Modern Latin American Fiction*. New York: Chelsea House Publishers, 1990.

Covington, Paula H., ed. *Latin America and the Caribbean: A Critical Guide to Research Sources*. Westport, CT: Greenwood, 1992.

González Echevarría, Roberto. *Myth and Archive: A Theory of the Latin American Narrative*. Durham, NC: Duke University Press, 1998.

González Echevarría, Roberto. *The Voice of the Masters: Writing and Authority in Modern Latin American Literature*. Austin: University of Texas Press, 1985.

González Echevarría, Roberto, and Enrique Pupo Walker, eds. *The Cambridge History of Latin American Literature*. 3 vols. New York: Cambridge University Press, 1996. Vol. 2 is on modern Latin American literature.

Hart, Stephen M. *A Companion to Latin American Literature*. London: Tamesis, 2007.

Henríquez Ureña, Pedro. *Literary Currents in Hispanic America*. Cambridge, MA: Harvard University Press, 1945.

Jrade, Cathy L. *Modernismo, Modernity, and the Development of Spanish American Literature*. Austin: University of Texas Press, 1998.

Kirkpatrick, Gwen. *The Dissonant Legacy of Modernismo: Lugones, Herrera y Reissig, and the Voices of Modern Spanish American Poetry*. Berkeley: University of California Press, 1989.

Luis, William, ed. *Modern Latin-American Fiction Writers*. First Series. Detroit: Gale, 1992.

Luis, William, and Ann González, eds. *Modern Latin-American Fiction Writers*. Second Series. Detroit: Gale, 1994.

Paz, Octavio. *Children of the Mire: Modern Poetry from Romanticism to the Avant-Garde*. Cambridge, MA: Harvard University Press, 1974.

Pérez Firmat, Gustavo, ed. *Do the Americas Have a Common Literature?* Durham, NC: Duke University Press, 1990.

Picón Salas, Mariano. *A Cultural History of Spanish America, from Conquest to Independence.* Translated by Irving A. Leonard. Berkeley: University of California Press, 1962.

Solé, Carlos A., ed. *Latin American Writers.* New York: Charles Scribner's Sons, 1989.

Unruh, Vicky. *Latin American Vanguards: The Art of Contentious Encounters.* Berkeley: University of California Press, 1994.

Index

Index

COLONIAL LATIN AMERICAN LITERATURE
A Very Short Introduction
Rolena Adorno

A vivid account of the literature of the Spanish-speaking Americas from the time of Columbus to Latin American Independence, this *Very Short Introduction* examines the origins of colonial Latin American literature in Spanish, the writings and relationships among major literary and intellectual figures of the colonial period, and the story of how Spanish literary language developed and flourished in a new context. Authors and works have been chosen for the merits of their writings, their participation in the larger debates of their era, and their resonance with readers today.

www.oup.com/uk/isbn/978-0-19-975502-8